PREPPER'S LIVESTOCK HANDBOOK

LIFESAVING STRATEGIES AND SUSTAINABLE METHODS FOR KEEPING CHICKENS, RABBITS, GOATS, COWS AND OTHER FARM ANIMALS

Leigh Tate

Ulysses Press

Published in the United States by:
Ulysses Press
P.O. Box 3440
Berkeley, CA 94703
www.ulyssespress.com

Printed in Canada by Marquis Book Printing
10 9 8 7 6 5 4 3 2 1

ISBN: 978-1-61243-795-8
Library of Congress Control Number: 2018930773

Acquisitions editor: Casie Vogel
Managing editor: Claire Chun
Project editor: Shayna Keyles
Editor: Renee Rutledge
Proofreader: Bill Cassel
Indexer: Sayre Van Young
Front cover and interior design: what!design @ whatweb.com
Cover artwork from shutterstock.com: wooden boards © Madredus, chickens © napocska, pigs © pavla, goat © suphanat
Interior artwork: see page 230

Distributed by Publishers Group West

To those who are willing to stay the course.
"Know well the condition of your flocks,
and pay attention to your herds;
for riches are not forever,
nor does a crown endure to all generations."

Proverbs 27:23-24

CONTENTS

INTRODUCTION

At midnight on January 1, 2000, my family gathered around the telephone and held their breath. It was Y2K. We had heeded the advice to prepare for a possible failure of the world's computer systems. We'd stocked up on canned and dried goods, water, kerosene lamps, kerosene, firewood, and a laundry plunger for washing clothes. At 12:01 a.m., my husband picked up the receiver and listened. We had a dial tone! The lights didn't go out, and life went on as usual.

Even though Y2K is a distant memory now, preparedness remains a trendy topic. Whether motivated by environmental, economic, political, or personal uncertainties, more and more people are taking steps to be prepared. Preparedness can take different forms. For some people, it might mean working from a checklist to stock up on enough food and supplies to last three months, six months, or even a year. Others, like Dan and I, choose a different approach—homesteading.

WHAT IS HOMESTEADING?

I think it's safe to say that homesteading means different things to different people. For some, it might be as simple as having a garden and keeping a few backyard chickens. For others, it may mean a full-scale off-grid lifestyle. Or it may mean something in between. The common ground is that homesteaders desire a simpler, more sustainable, more self-reliant way of living. They desire to be more hands-on in meeting their needs and the needs or their families. Homesteading describes the lifestyle that enables them to work toward this goal.

WHY HOMESTEAD?

If you absolutely love your job and your life, then likely, homesteading won't interest you. But there are reasons you might consider homesteading:

* You feel your life is too fast-paced and hectic.

* You don't like the pressure to have more, do more, and be more.

* You feel dissatisfied with consumerism and its ever-rising costs.

* You want to know exactly where your food comes from and what's in it.

* You have a sense of being disconnected from nature.

* You want your lifestyle to be more environmentally friendly.

* You feel that the world is heading in the wrong direction and you are uncertain about what the future holds.

Homesteading is the answer to all of these concerns and more. It's a choice that enables you to take steps toward greater independence and have a sense of purpose while taking them.

From a preparedness perspective, Dan and I believe that working toward self-reliance is our best strategy. While I admit we have little confidence in the current economic system and the lifestyle required to maintain it, I can also tell you that our self-reliance has been lifesaving on more fundamental levels. Many of you understand what it's like to be jobless for months, or to have an extended loss of power. Or perhaps you are looking at a limited-income retirement. For these reasons, we have found self-reliance to be prudent as well as practical.

WHO IS THIS BOOK FOR?

This book is for those who are looking for long-term preparedness that goes beyond simply stocking up on canned foods, dry goods, and other necessities. Gardening adds fresh vegetables and fruits to the diet, but keeping farm animals will enable you to have fresh eggs, milk, butter, cheese, and meat.

Those of us who didn't grow up farming are often puzzled about how to begin. We lack the skills and knowledge needed to make a start. Dan and I had to rely on research plus trial and error, but always with the question "what if?" on our minds. What if we could no longer buy layer pellets at the feed store? What if we could no longer buy filters for straining milk, or cultures and rennet for making cheese? What if the grid goes down—how will we store our eggs, milk, and meat? Some of what we tried worked, but some of it didn't. This book is a compilation of everything we have learned about preparedness with livestock and how we put it into practice. Its aim is to give you the advantage of our research and experience, so that hopefully you can avoid some of the problems we have had.

A truly comprehensive book on livestock preparedness would be nearly impossible to write. It would have to cover all farm animals in all locations, including variables in climate, seasons, weather, soil, and terrain. The truth of the matter is that what works well for one person in one part of the world may or may not work for someone in a different location.

Prepper's Livestock Handbook will give you the information you need to make workable choices for your own homestead. My goal is to give you a foundation upon which to build that you can adjust according to your personal goals and circumstances. In the Resources section, you will find lists to help you research your specific choices and needs. I recommend that you get a three-ring binder for organizing your personalized notes. Computers and digital devices are convenient, but hard-copy information will be there when electronics fail.

FIRST THINGS FIRST

People keep livestock for many reasons: eggs, dairy, meat, vegetation control, manure for compost, to sell, as pets, for showing, for breed conservation, because they like a particular animal, or any combination of these. Your reasons for keeping farm animals will determine your livestock philosophy and methods, as will your location and terrain.

Regional factors to consider include seasonal temperatures and length of daylight. Egg laying, for example, is influenced by the amount of daylight. Areas with mild winters will allow for year-round grazing, while colder areas with more snow will limit pasture and forage. Climates with harsh winters will require sturdier housing and wind breaks. In climates with sweltering summer heat, you will need to provide shade and plenty of fresh water. Breed choices may be affected by these conditions too. Long-haired Highland cattle will thrive in cold climates, while the Florida Cracker is well adapted to hot climates. Nubian and Savanna breed goats are more heat than cold tolerant, while Saanens and Oberhaslis adapt better to cold. Most animals will do well on any terrain, although rocks and steep hills will make fencing and barn building more challenging!

Country acreage offers the broadest possibilities for keeping livestock, but many mid- and small-size homesteads keep a variety of mid- and small-size animals to meet their family's needs. These include urban and suburban homesteads where people raise chickens, rabbits, and miniature breeds of goats and pigs.

Once you know your area, start researching livestock laws. The state, county, town (if you are within city limits), and homeowners association (if you have one) will all have something to say about what animals you can keep and how you can keep them. In urban and suburban areas, you will likely have limits on the kinds and numbers of animals you can keep; for example, you may be allowed up to three chickens (hens only) in your backyard. You may find that some animals can be kept as pets, such as rabbits, miniature pigs, or even miniature goats. In rural areas there are other laws you will need to know, such as fence laws. All states have a definition of a "legal fence." If your fencing doesn't meet those specifications, you may find yourself without legal recourse if your neighbor's goats break in and gobble down your garden.

Knowing what the law allows ahead of time can save a lot of headaches later on. However, even discouraging laws can be changed through proper channels. See Chapter 1 Resources on page 206 for some ideas on how to do that.

Next, evaluate the property itself. Here are some things to consider.

Animal housing. Cleared land, existing fences, and a barn will give you a head start toward acquiring your first critters. Or perhaps there are outbuildings that could be converted to animal housing? If you will need to build, check your local building codes first. Some folks say "it's easier to ask forgiveness than to get permission," but make sure you're able to pay potentially hefty fines to get that forgiveness.

A farm landscape with duck pond

Water sources. Does the property have a pond, spring, or well? Will you be buying from the municipal water supply? If a creek or river runs through or borders the property, check state laws regarding waterways and buffer areas. You may be prohibited from damming or diverting it, or your livestock may be forbidden access to it.

Regulation on sale of animal products. If you are considering livestock as part of your homestead income, you need to be aware of laws governing the sale of animal products for human consumption. The sale of milk and dairy products, for example, is highly regulated and will determine everything from your milking and milk-handling facilities to how the health of your animals is tested. Some states have cottage industry laws which allow the sale of homegrown eggs without a permit, while other states require certification. Selling animals for meat comes with its own set of rules. I'll discuss this in more detail in Chapter 7, Eggs, Milk, and Meat.

Locally available breeds. In your planning stages, I recommend researching what kinds and breeds of livestock are locally available. I spent many hours researching breeds of goats, only to discover that the breed I wanted wasn't available anywhere within several states of my location. By browsing local sales papers and websites, you can get a better sense of what's available, plus what you can expect to pay.

Local feed stores. Scout out local feed stores and feed mills for equipment, supplies, feeds, and farm seeds. Don't overlook the places where you do your family shopping. I can buy chicken feed, chicken scratch, and rabbit feed at my local grocery. Our Walmart even sells hog feed and horse wormer. Your county cooperative extension agent can be helpful as you get started, especially with information specific to your area.

Livestock vet. You will need to find a good livestock vet, one who specializes in large animals. Most veterinary practices are geared toward small pets and aren't always knowledgeable in the ailments and care of farm animals. Many of us with livestock have to do much of our own vetting, but a good vet is an invaluable resource. Also, a mentor is a great asset: someone with experience who is willing to answer questions and show you how to do things such as trim hoofs or give shots.

Stocking rates. Probably the most common questions are "How much land do I need?" and "How many animals can I keep on my property?" Called "stocking rates," the answers to those questions are often unsatisfying, because they depend not only on the amount of land but on the quality of forage, as well as the kinds of animals you want to keep. I will give you a better idea on that in the next chapter, Best Breeds for Self-Reliance.

CHAPTER 2

BEST BREEDS FOR SELF-RELIANCE

When Dan and I started looking for property, we spent many hours discussing what we would do with it. Livestock was a given, but what kind? What breed? It was fun to research the various farm animals and choose favorites. Over the years, we've had chickens, goats, rabbits, guinea fowl, ducks, pigs, and a llama. One of the things we have learned is that not all breeds of livestock are equally suited to the goals of self-reliance and preparedness.

Most of the livestock breeds that people are familiar with are commercial breeds. These are the animals we see on farms in the movies and in children's picture books. They are the most common breeds because industrialized agriculture is the most extensive form of farming practiced in the modern world. Commercial producers are looking for cost effectiveness: maximum output (profit) on the most economical inputs (expenses) possible. The breeds they use have been developed to increase production and weight gain on scientifically formulated feeds with the ability to tolerate overcrowding in confined spaces. Breeding and mothering instincts are considered nonessential and often bred out. Some commercial breeds of chickens and turkeys, for example, don't know how to mate and don't know how to hatch their eggs. Artificial insemination is used instead.

For the homesteader, there are other options. These include heritage breeds, crossbreeds, and dual-purpose breeds.

Heritage breeds. These are the old-fashioned farm animals that were expected to forage for themselves, be hardy, reproduce naturally, and raise their young with minimal problems. Their numbers have dwindled with the expansion of commercial farming, and many have become rare and hard to find. Thanks to the conservation efforts of enthusiastic breeders, sustainable farmers, and homesteaders, these breeds are beginning to thrive again. Depending on local availability or how far you're willing to travel to get them, heritage breeds might be an excellent choice for you.

Crossbreeds. These are usually less expensive, easier to find, and often, easier to care for. When breeders focus on improving selective traits in a particular breed, the gene pool becomes smaller. This increases the likelihood of the desired trait, but also increases the potential for inbred weaknesses. Hybrid vigor is often observed with crossbred animals, which are stronger and hardier than their purebred parents are. The downside to crossbreeds is that they can be harder to sell if the local market demands purebred animals.

Dual-purpose breeds. Livestock are typically classified by purpose: milk cows or beef cows; egg-laying or meat chickens, for example. A milk cow will give more milk than a beef cow, and a beef cow will have more muscle than a milker. This is true of layer and broiler chickens too. A dual-purpose animal, on the other hand, won't necessarily outproduce in either department, but will give a fair amount in both. Australorps and Rhode Island Reds are examples of dual-purpose chickens, and the Kinder is an excellent dual-purpose goat. On the other hand, if you eat meat and your dairy cow just gave you a bull calf, or your LaMancha doe just had twin bucklings, these are still well-suited for feeding your family.

Australorp chickens

The following sections will give you basic information about types and breeds of livestock to consider. The recommended acreage is on the generous side, but it will make a good starting point as you evaluate your pasture for the animals you've chosen. With all breeds, my advice is to start small. Their numbers will grow soon enough, and you'll have a much better experience if you keep things manageable. As you consider various breeds, talk with others who have them, but keep in mind that favorites vary because they are based on experience. One person's favorite may have been someone else's nightmare! Animal personalities and behaviors vary tremendously and don't always conform to the generalized breed description.

CATTLE

Hereford cow

If you have the acreage and a large family, then a cow may be a good choice for you. Cows produce lots of milk, which means lots of butter and cheese. Although a herd animal, a single cow will be content in a pasture by herself, more so than other herd animals. Cows are generally easier to contain, too, with a standard barbed-wire or board fence being adequate.

Here are a few other reasons to keep cattle:

* Manure for composting
* As draft animals
* Lawn mowing
* Hides for leather tanning
* Calves to trade or sell

Depending on your needs, you can choose a standard-size, midsize, or miniature cow. Below is some general information about each of these, including examples of breeds commonly kept as family cows.

All breeds listed below are heritage breeds except Brown Swiss, Hereford, Jersey, Belfair, and Zebu. Crossbred cattle are also a good option.

OVERVIEW OF COW BREEDS

	STANDARD SIZE	MIDSIZE	MINIATURE
HEIGHT	48 to 65 inches tall at the hips	42 to 48 inches tall at the hips	Typically smaller than 42 inches at the hips
WEIGHT	1,000 to 1,700 pounds	800 to 1,000 pounds	500 to 700 pounds
DAILY MILK PRODUCTION	6 to 10 gallons	2 to 5 gallons	1 to 4 gallons
ACREAGE REQUIRED	About 2 acres of good pasture for one cow (with or without a calf), more if your pasture is poor	Each midsize cow (or cow/calf pair) should have 1½ acres of good pasture, more if the pasture is poor	Miniatures should have at least 1 acre of good pasture for each cow
AVERAGE LIFESPAN	20 to 25 years	18 to 20 years	16 to 20 years
PRODUCTIVE LIFESPAN	10 to 14 years	10 to 12 years	10 to 12 years
DAIRY BREEDS	Guernsey, Holstein (the largest of the lot), Jersey (the smallest of the standard-size)	Kerry, some Jerseys	Miniature Jersey, Zebu
MEAT BREEDS	Hereford, Galloway, Belted Galloway, Texas longhorns	Texas longhorn (can grow larger than midsize), Florida Cracker	Miniature Hereford
DUAL-PURPOSE BREEDS	Brown Swiss, dual-purpose Shorthorns, (also called Milking Shorthorns), Dexter, Milking Devon, Red Poll, Randall	Pineywoods, Highland (sometimes called Scottish Highland) are considered a meat breed but can be milked	Dexter, Belfair

Holstein cow

Other Considerations

Cost. Cows usually cost in the thousands of dollars, with midsize and miniature breeds being the most expensive. Registered and purebred cows will be higher than unregistered and crossbred.

Breeding. You have several options:

* Keep your own bull (who will need his own quarters and pasture).

* Purchase or trade for stud service with a breeder or neighbor.

* Use artificial insemination (this will require the purchase of semen and a veterinarian's help).

Milk production. Production is seasonal. A cow must be dried off about two months before her next calf is born. Additionally, milk production varies both among breeds (Holsteins give the most, Jerseys the least) and among individuals. Two cows of the same breed may not give the same amount of milk.

Weight. Consider that in the event of your cow's death, you will need the manpower and equipment to move and bury the body. This is also true if you plan to do your own butchering.

GOATS

Boer goats

Goats are an affordable choice for those with less money or less acreage, who need less milk, or who can't digest cow's milk. Goats do better on weedy, brushy pastures and wooded areas than cows. Like cows, goats come in standard, midsize, and miniature sizes, although these categories aren't as well-defined as for cattle. Also like cattle, goat breeds are classified as either dairy or meat, with the Kinder and a few heritage breeds being truly dual-purpose. Even so, a meat goat can be milked, and a milk goat can be used for meat. The listed acreage can be considered a starting point.

Here are a few other reasons to keep goats:

* Manure for composting
* Brush clearing
* Kids to trade or sell
* As pack animals
* To pull carts
* As pets
* Hides for leather tanning

OVERVIEW OF GOAT BREEDS

	STANDARD SIZE	MIDSIZE	MINIATURE
HEIGHT	Typically 28 to 32 inches tall at the withers (shoulder)	20 to 28 inches at the withers (taller for bucks)	16 to 22 inches at the withers (taller for bucks)
WEIGHT	130 to 160 pounds depending on the breed and sex	80 or more pounds for does (125 pounds and up for bucks)	50 to 100 pounds
DAILY MILK PRODUCTION	½ to 2 gallons	½ gallon to over 1 gallon	1 quart to ½ gallon average
ACREAGE REQUIRED	Four goats per acre	Six per acre on good forage	Seven or eight minis per acre, depending on pasture quality
AVERAGE LIFESPAN	10 to 15 years	10 to 12 years	10 to 12 years
PRODUCTIVE LIFESPAN	8 to 12 years	8 to 10 years	8 to 10 years
DAIRY BREEDS	Nubian, LaMancha, Oberhasli, Saanen, Toggenburg (smallest of the standards)	Mini Nubian, Mini LaMancha, Mini Alpine, Mini Saanen (These "Minis" are crosses between standard sizes and Nigerian Dwarfs, true miniatures. These breeds are smaller than their standard counterparts)	Nigerian Dwarf
MEAT BREEDS	Boer, Kiko, Myotonic (Tennessee Fainting)		Pygmy
DUAL-PURPOSE BREEDS	Spanish	Arapawa, Kinder	

Kinder goats

Other Considerations

Cost. Expect to pay between $150 and $450 per goat depending on the sex, breed, and whether or not the animals are registered. Crossbred goats will be less expensive.

Breeding. The rule of thumb for first breeding standard-size does is eight months of age and 80 pounds in weight. You have several options for breeding goats:

* Keep your own buck (see Breeding and Pregnancy on page 92 for options).

* Purchase or trade for stud service with a breeder or neighbor.

* Use artificial insemination (this will require the purchase of semen and a veterinarian's help).

Milk production. Production is seasonal. A doe must be dried off about two months before kidding again. Year-round production is possible by either not breeding a doe in milk but allowing her to milk through to the following year, or by breeding does at different times of the year. Also, consider that the miniature breeds often have small teats, which can be difficult to milk by hand. The smallest of them can be too short to stand over a milking bucket.

Sociability. Goats are herd animals and extremely miserable without another goat.

Kids. Twins are most common, followed by singles and triplets. Kinders and Nigerian Dwarfs frequently have quadruplets. Bucklings can be fertile as young as two months of age.

SHEEP

East Friesian sheep

What do Roquefort, feta, and ricotta cheeses all have in common? They are traditionally made from sheep's milk! Sheep are usually raised for wool or meat, but for a small family farm or homestead, consider a breed that can provide milk as well. Sheep's milk is higher in milk solids, protein, and butterfat than either cow's or goat's milk. Although dairy sheep produce less milk than dairy goats, the higher protein content means it will yield more cheese than an equal volume of goat's or cow's milk.

Here are some other reasons to keep sheep:

* Manure for compost
* Pets
* Lambs to trade or sell
* Pelts
* Lawn mowing

Sheep vary in size but are not categorized that way. They are categorized according to purpose and the kind of wool they produce (meat, dairy, long wool, medium wool, fine wool, etc.). Here, I'll give general information about sheep and then list examples of dairy and dual-purpose breeds.

As mammals, sheep produce milk for their young, but the dairy sheep breeds produce milk for about eight months compared to nondairy sheep, which will produce for three to five months. They can also be shorn for their wool, making them dual-purpose.

OVERVIEW OF SHEEP BREEDS

HEIGHT	24 to 42 inches or so, depending on sex and breed
WEIGHT	From 75 to 125 pounds for the smallest breeds (Shetland and Babydoll Southdown) to 150 to 300 pounds for the larger breeds
DAILY MILK PRODUCTION	1½ to 2½ quarts, less for nondairy breeds
ACREAGE REQUIRED	Five per acre on good pasture
LIFESPAN	10 to 15 years
PRODUCTIVE LIFESPAN	The best practice for breeding young ewes is at around 18 months of age. Typically, ewes are retired at around seven years old, but can produce longer if well cared for.
MEAT AND WOOL BREEDS	Romeldale, California Variegated Mutant (CVM), Black Welsh Mountain, Cotswold, Leicester Longwool, Navajo-Churro, Southdown
MILK BREEDS	Lacaune, East Friesian
MILK AND WOOL BREEDS	Karakul, Shropshire
MILK, WOOL, AND MEAT BREEDS	Clun Forest, Tunis, Dorset

Other Considerations

Cost. One sheep will cost in the hundreds of dollars depending on the sex, breed, and whether or not it's registered. Crossbreeds will be less expensive.

Breeding. You have several options:

❋ Keep your own ram (see Breeding and Pregnancy on page 92 for options).

❋ Purchase or trade for stud service with a breeder or neighbor.

❋ Use artificial insemination (tis will require the purchase of semen and a veterinarian's help).

Sociability. Sheep are herd animals, so you will need more than one.

Shearing. If your sheep grow a wool coat, they *must* be sheared at least once a year. Overgrown fleece becomes matted and can get caught in brambles, branches, and brush. Some breeds such as Shetlands naturally shed their winter coats. These can be removed by hand (called rooing).

PIGS

Tamworth pig and piglets

Of all the critters we've kept on our homestead, pigs have been a favorite. For our small acreage, we chose a small heritage breed, the American Guinea Hog. This friendly breed is an excellent pasture pig and forager, plus they turn almost any food waste into compost-ready manure, and are excellent natural tillers of the soil. Pigs are also good to keep for:

❋ Piglets to trade or sell

❋ Pets

❋ Hides for tanning

❋ Disposal of all butchering waste (including bones)

Pigs are classified as either meat/bacon or lard producers, with both commercial and heritage breeds to consider. Meat/bacon breeds tend to be lean, long-bodied, and fast growing, while the lard breeds are short-bodied with slower growth rates and good layers of fat. However, there is something of a spectrum here, and you will certainly get lard from a meat breed just as you will get meat from a lard breed. Some people talk about dual-purpose pigs, although this isn't an official category. Sometimes it refers to both meat and bacon, or sometimes it refers to meat plus lard. I've included a dual-purpose category here, which lists breeds homesteaders use for meat, bacon, and lard.

OVERVIEW OF PIG BREEDS

HEIGHT	22 to 36 inches at the shoulder, depending on breed
WEIGHT	As low as 150 pounds for the smallest females and up to 800 pounds for the largest males
ACREAGE REQUIRED	Recommendations vary, but 5 to 10 sows per acre is a good starting point.
NATURAL LIFESPAN	If well taken care of pigs can live to be 10 years and older.
PRODUCTIVE LIFESPAN	Gilts (maiden females) have their first heats between five and eight months old, but usually aren't bred until they are eight months. Commercial breeders retire sows after their seventh litter, but home breeders can expect eight or nine productive years.
MEAT AND BACON BREEDS	Yorkshire, Tamworth, Berkshire, Hampshire, Gloucestershire Old Spots (a meat breed with plenty of lard), Red Wattle (docile but large)
LARD BREEDS	American Guinea Hog, Ossabaw Island, Mulefoot, Vietnamese Pot-bellied, Chester White, Mangalitsa
MEAT, BACON, AND LARD BREEDS	Berkshire, Hampshire, Large Black, Guinea Hog, Gloucestershire Old Spots

Other Considerations

Cost. Depending on the time of year and breed, one pig can cost anywhere between $50 and several hundred dollars, with registered purebred animals being the most expensive.

Breeding. You have several options:

❋ Keep your own boar (see Breeding and Pregnancy on page 92 for options).

❋ Purchase or trade for stud service with a breeder or neighbor.

❋ Use artificial insemination (this will require the purchase of semen and a veterinarian's help).

Sociability. Most breeds don't necessarily need another pig, but if you want quick weight gain, consider more than one for food competition.

Wallows. Pigs love water and mud, especially during hot weather. If you don't offer them a mud wallow, they will likely make their own by knocking over the water bucket!

RABBITS

New Zealand white rabbits

Rabbits are an excellent option for any homestead. They provide meat, manure, and more rabbits—they make great pets, too. They can be raised in any backyard, garage, basement, or spare room. Rabbits are also good for pelts.

Rabbits are classified in several different ways: body type, fur type, weight, or purpose. Purpose categories include fancy (for showing and pets), breeding, meat, textiles (angora fiber), and research. Because we are approaching rabbits from a preparedness point of view, I'll just discuss the meat breeds.

OVERVIEW OF RABBIT BREEDS

LENGTH	Up to 20 inches
WEIGHT	Meat breeds range from 8 to 12 pounds as adults
OUTDOOR SPACE REQUIRED	Rabbits don't need acreage, but thrive best with an exercise yard. In addition to housing, plan on providing 32 square feet per rabbit for exercise.
NATURAL LIFESPAN	12 years or longer
PRODUCTIVE LIFESPAN	Large breed does (female rabbits) are typically bred for the first time between eight and twelve months of age. Depending on the preferences of the breeder, a doe in good condition can have four litters per year.
BREEDS	Champagne d'Argent, Creme d'Argent, Californian, American Chinchilla, Cinnamon, New Zealand, Palomino, Satin

Other Considerations

Cost. $5 to $50 per rabbit, depending on breed.

Breeding. You can either keep your own buck (male), or purchase or trade for stud service with a breeder or neighbor.

POULTRY

Chickens are commonly the first farm animal people get when they start homesteading. But there are other choices for poultry, and many folks keep a variety. All can be used for eggs and meat.

Chickens

White Leghorn hens

Commercial egg and meat breeds are usually hybrids, which produce more than heritage breeds but also eat more and aren't as well adapted to foraging. Broiler types produce those plump grocery store chicken breasts, but they are not a good option for preppers because they are very poor at reproduction.

Free-range birds still need a chicken yard or run for the times you need to keep them out of the pasture. Some folks use a chicken tractor and move it about to provide fresh forage. It is worth noting that some breeds are better suited to confinement than others are. In Resources, you'll find web links to several charts comparing the various breeds and their characteristics. Indoor space requirements will be discussed in the next chapter, and breeding will be discussed in Chapter 5.

Here are some other reasons to raise chickens:

* Pets (if hand raised from chicks)
* Ornamental (especially the colorful and fancy breeds)
* Manure for the compost bin
* Extra eggs, chicks, and adult birds to trade or sell
* Feathers for crafts

OVERVIEW OF CHICKEN BREEDS

	STANDARD SIZE	MINIATURE (BANTAM)
WEIGHT	4 to 10 pounds	1 to 2 pounds
OUTDOOR SPACE REQUIREMENTS	Minimum of 8 to 10 square feet per bird	4 square feet per bantam
NATURAL LIFESPAN	10 to 12 years	10 to 12 years
PRODUCTIVE LIFESPAN	1 + years	1 + years
EGG-LAYING BREEDS	White Leghorn, Black Australorp, Ameraucana (Easter Eggers), Speckled Sussex	Same as standard size
MEAT-PRODUCING BREEDS	Brahma, Jersey Giant, Cochin, Langsham	Same as standard size
FANCY BREEDS	Crevecoeur, Lakenvelder, Polish	Silky
DUAL-PURPOSE BREEDS	Rhode Island Red, Wyandottes, Marans, Plymouth Rocks, Buff Orpingtons, New Hampshire Red, Delaware	Same as standard size

Other Considerations

Land use. Chickens can be quite hard on the land and will rearrange mulch and compost quickly. Plan to rotate their areas as you do with larger livestock.

Productive lifespan. Commercial breeders typically keep their layers no more than a year or two, and then replace them. The rationale is that egg production peaks the first year and rapidly drops after that. From a homesteading perspective, however, pastured chickens have a much longer production life. Most will continue to produce well for four or more years.

Ducks

Muscovy ducks

We never considered ducks for the homestead because we don't have a pond. When I was offered Muscovy ducks in trade for a Guinea Hog piglet, however, I reconsidered. I was told they didn't need much water and were quiet. Quiet ducks! Yes, it's true, and they're happy with a wading pool for water. Ducks are commonly kept for eggs, meat, or both. They're also good for:

⚜ Pets (if hand raised from ducklings)

⚜ Ornamental, especially the colorful and unusual breeds

⚜ Manure for the compost pile

⚜ Extra eggs, ducklings, and adult birds to trade or sell

⚜ Feathers for crafts

⚜ Down for pillows and bedding

Ducks for homesteading can be classified as egg layers, meat types, or dual-purpose. Egg-laying ducks, particularly Indian Runners and several types of Campbells, actually lay more eggs than the most productive chicken breeds—anywhere between 250 and 325 eggs per year. Egg-layers tend to be smaller in size, and meat breeds lay the least. Dual-purpose ducks are a compromise.

OVERVIEW OF DUCK BREEDS

WEIGHT	Egg-layers: 3 to 6 pounds Meat breeds: 9 to 15 pounds Dual purpose: 5 to 7 pounds
OUTDOOR SPACE REQUIREMENTS	Minimum 15 square feet per duck for a run or yard; more is better
NATURAL LIFESPAN	8 to 12 years
PRODUCTIVE LIFESPAN	Egg production is highest in the first three to five years, but can continue at a reduced rate for eight years or longer.
EGG-LAYING BREEDS	Indian Runners, Campbells, Mallards
MEAT-PRODUCING BREEDS	Pekin, Muscovy
DUAL-PURPOSE BREEDS	Ancona, Buff Orpington, Welsh Harlequin, Swedish (Blue and Black)

Other considerations

❋ Campbells are winter layers.

❋ Muscovies and Mallards are fliers. Muscovies like to roost in trees.

❋ Muscovy meat is less fatty than other duck breeds and is often likened in flavor to beef.

❋ Duck eggs are richer than chicken eggs and highly prized by gourmet chefs for baking.

❋ Duck fat also has gourmet appeal.

Turkeys

Narragansett turkey

Turkey undoubtedly holds a place of honor in the holiday meal hall of fame. It's also considered an excellent substitute for beef and pork. Turkey eggs are edible too, and considered similar to chicken eggs in flavor. Turkeys are also great for:

⚜ Manure for the compost pile

⚜ Feathers for crafts

⚜ Extra poults and adults to sell or trade

When selecting turkeys, choices include commercial (production) or heritage breeds. The commercial types are the broad-breasted breeds, which show rapid growth rates and produce large meaty breasts. These are not suitable as self-sustaining breeds, however, because they require artificial insemination to produce eggs. Heritage breeds are slower growing but able to mate naturally, raise their own young (called poults), and forage. Depending on the breed, turkey hens lay between 60 and 120 eggs per year. White turkeys have the whitest skin for a visually appealing roast turkey.

OVERVIEW OF TURKEY BREEDS

WEIGHT	20 to 35 pounds for males, 15 to 20 pounds for females
OUTDOOR SPACE REQUIREMENTS	Allow a minimum of 20 square feet per turkey in your yard or run.
NATURAL LIFESPAN	About 10 years
PRODUCTIVE LIFESPAN	Hens produce well for five to seven years.
HERITAGE BREEDS	Black Spanish, Blue Slate, Standard Bronze, Bourbon Red, Midget White, Narragansett, Royal Palm, White Holland

Geese

Geese are primarily raised for meat but also for their eggs, with one goose egg equaling three from a chicken. They make good watch animals, as they announce the approach of strange people and animals and stand their ground against small predators, such as foxes and hawks. Geese are also raised for:

* Feather and down production
* Weed control
* Source of high-quality fat
* Manure for the compost
* Entertainment
* Pets
* Excess eggs, goslings, and adult geese to sell or trade

If you're thinking of keeping geese, keep these things in mind:

* Geese are commonly loud and noisy!
* Geese are primarily grass eaters.
* Some can be aggressive, particularly the ganders during breeding season.
* Droppings are messy and bountiful.
* Geese prefer open spaces (free ranging) to coops and enclosures.
* Geese are waterfowl and are happiest when provided at least a small pool of water.

OVERVIEW OF GEESE BREEDS

	LIGHT	MEDIUM	HEAVY
WEIGHT	10 to 12 pounds	13 to 17 pounds	18 to 26 pounds
OUTDOOR SPACE REQUIREMENTS	Minimum 18 square feet per goose for a run or yard; more is better	Minimum 18 square feet per goose for a run or yard; more is better	Minimum 18 square feet per goose for a run or yard; more is better
NATURAL LIFESPAN	15 to 20 years or longer	15 to 20 years or longer	15 to 20 years or longer
PRODUCTIVE LIFESPAN	Spring after hatching to well into teenage years, laying 10 to 25 eggs per year	Spring after hatching to well into teenage years, laying 10 to 25 eggs per year	Spring after hatching to well into teenage years, laying 10 to 25 eggs per year
HERITAGE BREEDS	Chinese, Roman	Pilgrim, American Buff, Pomeranian, Sebastopol	African, Toulouse, Embden

Guinea Fowl

Guinea fowl

I first bought guinea fowl keets after losing one of our livestock guardian dogs to Lyme disease. It had been a terrible year for ticks and it was a blow to lose him. We kept the guineas only one year, but they were my favorite of the various poultry we've had. Besides being wonderfully entertaining, they did an excellent job of eradicating our ticks. Unfortunately, there is no such thing as quiet guinea fowl. Guineas are alarmists and they are noisy! They are considered good "watchdogs" because they will alert you to anything happening in your yard, your neighbor's yard, or your neighbor's neighbor's yard.

Guineas are classified by color and provide delicious eggs and meat. Other great reasons to keep guinea fowl include:

* Pets
* Feathers for crafts
* Manure for compost
* Extra eggs, keets, and birds to sell or trade
* Ornamental
* Entertainment

OVERVIEW OF GUINEA FOWL BREEDS

WEIGHT	2.5 to 4 pounds
OUTDOOR SPACE REQUIREMENTS	Guineas prefer free ranging. They are fliers, however, and not inclined to stay where the humans think they should stay.
NATURAL LIFESPAN	10 to 15 years
PRODUCTIVE LIFESPAN	Guineas are seasonal layers, and usually start laying the spring after they were hatched. Productivity begins to drop when they reach four or five years of age.
BREEDS	Pearl, White, Lavender, Buff Purple, Coral Blue

Other Considerations

Training. One problem with guinea fowl is that they dislike roosting indoors at night. This makes them easy pickings for owls, foxes, coyotes, etc. To train them, they must be kept indoors for at least six weeks. This is how long it takes to develop their roosting habits. They can be trained to come when called with proso millet. They love millet and will come running any time they know you have this treat.

Other Considerations for All Types of Poultry

Cost. Prices range from a couple of dollars each for chicks, to $5 to $12 each for ducklings, goslings, keets, and poults.

Purchasing. Options include buying eggs for hatching (requires an incubator or surrogate broody hen), day-old babies, or grown birds. Mail ordering from hatcheries is a common way of buying poultry. They offer the greatest variety of breeds and usually guarantee disease-free stock, but require a minimum number of birds per order plus other handling charges in addition to two-day shipping. Local feed stores often sell baby poultry, usually chicks and ducklings purchased from commercial hatcheries. This enables you to buy only what you need rather than a minimum order. The other option is buying locally from someone with a surplus to sell or trade. If you do purchase poultry locally, ask about problems the seller has had with their flock. Do not buy poultry from flocks with disease problems.

Chicks and ducklings can be purchased as "straight run" or sexed. Straight run is you-get-what-you-get, theoretically half males and half females, but oftentimes the balance is in favor of the males. Sexed chicks or ducklings are not 100 percent guaranteed, but the vast majority will be what you order. All females will cost more than all males or straight run. Other kinds of poultry are usually sold straight run only.

Breeding. You will need to keep a male if you want home-hatched poultry. Egg production, however, does not require fertilization, so you can still have eggs with an all-female flock. If you want to increase your numbers or replace older hens, you can use either an incubator or a broody hen to hatch out purchased fertile eggs. Broody hens also make good surrogate mothers to purchased chicks.

Mixed Flocks. Can you keep various species of birds in a common poultry house and yard? Many people keep mixed flocks successfully with no problems, but some sources warn against the practice. Objections range from disease risks and mating problems to feeding and nutritional considerations. My experience of keeping multispecies flocks falls in the camp of successful experiences.

CHAPTER 3

BARNS, SHELTERS, AND FENCING

When Dan and I started preparing for livestock, we wondered if one of our two small outbuildings would be adequate shelter for chickens and goats. We made several modifications on what became our first "barn." We learned a lot from that setup and from the animals too. We made a number of changes over the years, and when we finally built a chicken coop and a goat barn, we were able to build structures that met both their needs and ours.

Proper shelter and good fencing are two important aspects of preparing for livestock, and as you'll see in this chapter, you have a lot of options. They can be expensive, but as a one-time cost, it is well worth getting the best you can afford.

In the following pages, I'll discuss basic livestock housing along with a few ideas to help you design shelter to meet your goals and needs. I'll share fencing options with you, including the things we wish we'd known before we started on ours.

MEETING BASIC NEEDS

Animals need protection from wind, rain, snow, hot sun, and predators. A good structure is not overcrowded or damp. It provides good ventilation, and is draft free. Location is also important. High ground with good drainage is a must. Shade and wind breaks are helpful. A structure that is centrally located on your property will enable you to rotate where your animals are allowed to graze and roam. It should be close enough to the house to make it convenient to tend them, but not so close so that their squawking, mooing, baaing, and bleating are too noisy for you or your neighbors. Or too smelly. If you're going to keep a bull, buck, or ram, you will need a way to separate it until breeding time. For most of us, that means separate quarters and a separate paddock. Proximity to property lines may be stipulated in your state or county building codes.

How big does it need to be? That depends on how many animals you want to keep and what you can afford for materials. Here are several options, along with minimal space requirements for individual species. In Resources, I list where to find specific plans.

TYPES OF LIVESTOCK STRUCTURES

Nothing says "farm" like a barn. It is the working center of the farm, built to house livestock, feed, hay, and equipment. If your property came with a barn or outbuildings and fencing, consider yourself fortunate. Shelters and fencing are expensive to build. If you need to build from the ground up you have some work to do, but you will have the opportunity to plan things out and custom build according to your needs. Listed here are some shelter options to consider.

Large traditional barn. This will take more time and money to build, but has the convenience of keeping everything under one roof. Each group of animals has its own area, often with their own entry. If the barn is centrally located to your pastures, rotational grazing is easy to manage.

Traditional barn

Chicken coop

Smaller species-specific structures. For example, we have a chicken coop, doe barn, buck barn for permanent housing, and three-sided goat shelter to provide a dry shady area when the goats are in our farthest paddock. The advantage to these is that they can be built as needed and located wherever you want those animals to be.

Open structures. A good structure doesn't have to have four walls, especially if strategically placed windbreaks are provided. Open structures are often used as loafing areas, but depending on your climate an open structure for sun and rain protection may be all that you need. Or, a three-sided structure can be suitable if the open side faces away from the prevailing winds in your area.

Portable structures. Portable structures are popular and can be used for other livestock as well. They can be built on skids and relocated as part of a rotational grazing plan or wherever you need sun and rain protection. Chicken tractors are an example of a portable structure.

Temporary structures. These are usually hoop-type houses that can be set up anywhere and relocated as needed. They are a good way to provide shelter from rain or hot sun without having to bring your animals back to the barn. We've used them to store hay and as a seasonal pig shelter.

Space Requirements

When considering how big your structure needs to be, the following guidelines are helpful. These are minimums listed as square feet per individual animal. More is better, especially if your animals will spend a lot of time indoors. Cramped animals become stressed animals and will display more health and behavioral problems than those with adequate space. Recommendations vary according to source, but in general, I would be comfortable with the following:

Cattle: 75 to 100 square feet

Chickens: 4 to 5 square feet

Ducks: 4 to 5 square feet

Geese: 6 square feet

Goats: 20 to 25 square feet

Guinea fowl: 4 square feet

Pigs: 50 square feet

Rabbits: 12 square feet

Sheep: 20 to 25 square feet

Turkeys: 6 square feet

DESIGNING YOUR STRUCTURE

A good design meets both the animals' needs and yours. To do that, here are some additional things you might want to consider.

Stalls

Many old floor plans of barns show individual stalls for each animal, but are separate stalls necessary? They are advantageous if you need to work with individual animals, but you will also need as many water buckets and hay feeders as stalls, so consider the added workload.

I use stalls only for specific reasons, so a few permanent or even temporary stalls work well:

Introducing new animals. Keeping them separate but able to see and smell one another is helpful for introducing new livestock to your existing herd or flock. Breeders of registered animals sometimes keep new stock separate to test for particular diseases before allowing them to mingle.

Birthing and bonding. I find this especially important for my first-time mothers. They are often amazed and aren't sure about letting their babies nurse. Giving the new mother a place to become accustomed to the baby's smell and her new role is helpful.

Isolating sick animals. This is a must to reduce the risk of spreading disease.

Multispecies Housing

Can various species share the same quarters? I was able to successfully house my llama and livestock dogs with my goats, but feeding time and meeting mineral needs are easier to manage if each species has its own area. We've tried to keep poultry in separate areas, but they all prefer the chicken coop. They work out their respective places in the overall pecking order, and so far, we've had no problems with their chosen arrangement.

Flooring

This is a question folks ask about, so I'll give you some pros and cons for each type of flooring.

Dirt. Cheap and easy, nothing to install. Good drainage around the building site will prevent problems during extreme rainfall. If you plan to use deep litter (more on that below) then a dirt floor is best.

Concrete. Our first chicken coop and goat stall had concrete floors, but only because the concrete was already there. On the plus side, these floors were easy to clean with a flat-nose shovel and a garden hose. The negative was that ours didn't drain properly, so urine had no place to go. Concrete can be hard on the legs and cause hoof problems, even with daily cleaning, so plenty of bedding is important.

Pavers. Like concrete, pavers can be hard on the legs, so thick straw or rubber mats are commonly used on both concrete and paver floors.

Sand. People with sand floors really like them. The sand will absorb urine, but it will have to be replaced from time to time.

Wood. Even treated wood will withstand only so much moisture from urine and manure. Eventually it will rot out and need to be replaced. Best for storage areas.

Lighting and Ventilation

A light and airy shelter is by far the healthiest housing for all your livestock.

Light can include natural light from windows or skylights, or electrical lighting. I use solar-powered barn lights. These come with their own small solar panel and battery. See Resources on page 206 for more information.

Ventilation is a must. Animal digestion, breathing, and excreting of waste are all natural processes producing gases that are unhealthy if allowed to accumulate. Hay and straw add dust to the air. Without proper ventilation, animals become sick and die.

Ventilation can be natural or mechanical. Windows and vents in gable ends, eaves, and ridges facilitate air circulation. Fans can help too, and solar electric vent fans are a good preparedness option.

Heating and Cooling

If you live with extremely cold winter temperatures, you may wonder whether your shelter needs to be heated. Animals are able to withstand cold provided they have shelter from drafts and precipitation and plenty to eat. Without these, they will require significantly more calories to stay warm. For cattle, goats, and sheep, that means plenty of long-stemmed hay. Providing heat in the barn may actually be detrimental because it will prevent them from growing their winter coats. For pigs and rabbits, straw bedding should be thick enough to burrow into. For poultry, select breeds that are cold tolerant and will winter well. The deep litter system discussed in the next section is one way to provide warmth naturally.

If you live in an extremely hot climate, you may wonder about keeping your animals cool. Make sure they have easy access to shade and plenty of fresh water. Some people use large electric barn fans to keep air circulating. Pigs will keep cool in a mud wallow, and for rabbits, you can provide plastic 2-liter bottles of ice. For poultry, select breeds that are heat tolerant.

Loafing Areas

Horses outside a loafing shed

A traditional loafing shed is a three-sided structure offering shade and shelter from wind and rain. Where winters are mild, they can be used in place of a barn. If your summers are especially hot, an open carport-like structure serves well for shade. Some loafing sheds are built on skids so they can be moved as the stock is moved. An alternative to a separate loafing shed is a lean-to roof attached to the barn like an open porch. This serves to enlarge summer quarters and protects the doorway from rain and mud.

Feeding Areas

People approach feeding in different ways. Some put out pans to share, some use feeding troughs, and others use individual feeders. When using pans or troughs, it's helpful to separate young animals from adults, and pregnant and milking animals from non-producing ones. This way you can address the feed requirements of each group.

Community pans. These are probably the easiest way to go, and you won't need a separate feeding area. I can tell you from experience, however, that the animals highest in the social order get dibs on the feed and will chase or push the weaker and younger animals out of the way. One workaround is to divide the feed into as many pans as there are animals. Once they figure out that each pan contains the same thing, they'll settle down to eat. The fastest eaters will get the most, however, so monitor the condition of your animals to make sure everyone is getting enough to eat.

Community feeding pan

Feeding troughs. These work best if they are long enough to accommodate more animals than you have. Feed must be distributed evenly in the feeder, although the fastest eaters will soon clear their spots and push their neighbors out of the way. As with pan feeding, it is a good idea to monitor the condition of individual animals.

Pigs at feeding trough

Individual feeders. These work best if the animals can be tied in their places. I find that once my goats learn the routine, they each go stand by their own feeding spot when it's time to eat. This is by far the most peaceful way to feed and ensures that each animal gets its full ration.

Creep feeders. Commonly used for calves, lambs, piglets, and baby poultry, these are designed with small entrances for young animals while keeping larger animals out. They are useful because the young have higher nutritional needs than adults and are usually fed high-protein feed with supplemental calcium.

Feeder inside housing. This is usually done with poultry and rabbits.

Feed and Equipment Storage

You will need a feed and supply storage area, somewhere the animals can't get to. How large it needs to be will depend in part on how much feed you want to store. A 32-gallon trash can will hold 150 pounds of grain. If you use 50 pounds per week and want to store 12 weeks' worth, you will need enough room for four trash cans. A 55-gallon drum can hold about 200 pounds of grain but doesn't take up any more room than a trash can. Four drums, then, would hold 16 weeks' worth of grain.

Equipment will include any supplies that you need for routine care of your livestock. See Chapter 6, Blessed Events, and Chapter 8, Keeping Them Healthy, for several basic lists. Old cabinets and shelving work well for storing supplies.

Water

Running water isn't necessary in the barn if you don't mind hauling buckets. The options for running water include running a water line to the barn, or rainwater catchment. Art Ludwig's *Water Storage: Tanks, Cisterns, Aquifers, and Ponds* has helped us with our own catchment systems.

Winter presents the challenge of keeping livestock water ice-free. During a fairly mild winter, you may find it sufficient to keep water buckets in the barn. We fill ours with hot water in the morning and insulate them by placing them inside a larger container filled with straw. Electric water buckets are available, but off-grid options also exist: solar stock tank heaters, motion detector water pumping systems, solar-heated waterers, and earth-heated (geothermal) waterers. These can be either purchased or DIY. (See Resources on page 206 for where to find more information.)

Hay Feeders

Cows, goats, sheep, pigs, and rabbits all eat hay. Some farmers feed hay by tossing bales onto the ground, but this method is pretty wasteful because much of the hay is trampled. Hay that has been trampled isn't edible, so a hay feeder will reduce waste. The height of the feeder must make it accessible to whatever animals are feeding from it.

There are several possibilities for feeding hay.

Ground hay feeders. Built on or close to the ground so that the animal can eat in a natural grazing position, some have a bottom, but some are simply enclosures to keep the hay from being trampled. If built outdoors, you risk losing hay that rots on wet ground.

Ground hay feeder

Hay feeders. Also called hay racks or mangers, these are often V-shaped and large enough to hold a square bale or loose hay. They keep hay off the ground and are usually head height to the animal being fed. To minimize waste, some have a bottom or tray that

Hay net

extends out from the point of the V. This catches dropped hay and can double as a grain feeder.

Hay bags. These are hanging bags, usually canvas, with an opening at one end for accessing the hay. They are usually used in individual stalls.

Hay nets. These are similar to hay bags, but the netting has large enough openings that the animal can eat the hay through them. Nets and bags are a good option for a temporary setup.

Round bale feeders. Also known as ring feeders, these are large enough to hold a large, round bale of hay.

Hay Storage

Hay lofts are traditional but there are other ways to store hay. Some people use large sheds or tunnels. Some leave it out in the open. Dan and I prefer to store our hay under cover, because hay protected from sun bleaching and rain will retain the highest nutritional value and palatability. We've experimented with tarped piles on the ground, in a hoop house with a wood floor, and in a carport on concrete. But the ground was damp after rain and the concrete would sweat, so I wouldn't recommend either of those options.

How large will your hay storage area need to be? If you have a reliable source for hay, you have the option of storing small quantities and buying as needed. If you would like to calculate storage for enough hay to last the winter, then the following are *rough* estimates of hay needs for large livestock. Specific amounts depend on the kind of animals, how many, their weight and working condition (pregnant, milking, or dry), plus weather conditions, available forage, and the quality and moisture content of the hay. The following are based on a percentage of the average body weight of adult animals (see Chapter 4, Forage and Feed, for more information).

* Cattle: 1 ton per month per cow
* Goats: 150 pounds per month per goat
* Sheep: 225 pounds per month per sheep
* Pigs: 55 pounds per month per pig

If you plan to keep a donkey or llama as a livestock guardian (see Chapter 9, Keeping Them Safe, for more information on these), you can include the following:

❋ Donkey: 150 pounds per month per donkey

❋ Llama: 150 pounds per month per llama

How does this translate to a volume for hay? There is a great deal of variation in bale sizes and weights. Find out what bale sizes are locally available and use the following to estimate the space required.

❋ Traditional small square bales vary from 14 × 18 × 36 inches to 24 × 24 × 48 inches and weigh 40 to 75 pounds.

❋ Standard round bales vary from 4 × 4 feet to 5 × 5 feet and can vary in weight from 600 to 1000 pounds.

❋ Loose stacks aren't as compact and will require more room.

Milking and Milk Handling Areas

A separate milking area is useful, but not necessary. Some people simply tie up the animal to be milked (either indoors or out) and have at it. Milk straining and refrigeration are done in the house.

A milking stand or stanchion is very helpful for milking goats or smaller cows. These not only get the animal to a more comfortable milking height, but also include a feeder and head gate to keep her in her place. You can buy metal stanchions or make one yourself with wood. See Resources for where to find plans.

If you wish to sell milk, you will need to build your milking room and milk-handling facility in compliance with your local and state laws.

Cleaning and Manure Management

There are two commonly used methods for cleaning out a barn: daily or deep litter.

Daily cleaning out (also called "mucking out") is just what it says: the daily removal of manure and urine-soaked bedding and replacing it with fresh.

Deep litter is popular because it's less work. It starts with a good 4- to 6-inch layer of straw, wood chips, wood shavings, dried grass, or dried leaves; anything that won't clump and cake when wet. As urine and manure accumulate, add another 2-inch layer of bedding material. Stir occasionally to keep the litter loose and to introduce oxygen to promote decomposition and prevent unpleasant odors. As the bedding decomposes, it fosters beneficial microbes and produces heat. The result is a slow-working compost, which makes for warm bedding during cold weather. Deep litter can accumulate several feet in depth or more before cleaning out is necessary. A good 6 to 12 inches is left as a starter base for the next batch.

Does it contribute to disease amongst livestock? Quite the contrary. Studies at the Ohio Agricultural Experiment Station in the 1940s and '50s showed that poultry on deep litter gained more weight on less feed, and chicks had fewer deaths from coccidiosis, a life-threatening parasite problem.

FENCES

It is said that good fences make for good neighbors. When it comes to animals, that is certainly true! Fences will keep your pets and livestock from roaming onto the street or your neighbor's property. More than once, we've had someone knock at our door to tell us, "Your pig is running down the road!" Fences will also keep other animals off your property, which is particularly important for stray dogs and wild predators. To avoid potential disputes over fences, it's helpful to know how your state laws define a "lawful fence," particularly for boundary fences.

We've learned a lot about fencing and fencing materials over the years. For example, not all types of fencing are equally appropriate for all species of livestock. Some kinds of fences are probably more popular in your area than others, which will somewhat limit your choices. Fencing can be categorized as either permanent or temporary. Boundary fences define the perimeter of your property and should comply with your state's definition of a legal fence. Cross fencing divides large areas into smaller ones.

Wood Fencing

A traditional wood rail fence, which is also called a board fence, is aesthetic, but expensive. The boards will need to be spaced close enough to keep your stock in and unwanted animals out. Boards

Wood fencing

must be replaced from time to time, because even treated lumber will eventually rot out. Best suited for cattle.

Wire Fencing

There are several kinds of wire fencing: barbed, high tensile, welded, woven, knotted, poultry netting, no climb, and chain link. They are used as permanent fencing.

Barbed wire fences consist of two or more strands of barbed wire. Because of its barbs, this kind of fencing is difficult to work with. Best suited for cattle.

Barbed wire fence

High-tensile wire fences are usually 11- to 14-gauge wire and are easier to work with than barbed wire. Often used with an electric hot wire to deter predators. Best suited for cattle.

Welded wire fences are popular because they are economical. This is the kind of fencing we first used, but after several years of experience, I would not recommend it for livestock. The welds can pop, and animals pushing or rubbing on it can bend it out of shape. A hot wire run about goat-chest or pig-nose height would help. Not recommended for poultry, because hatchlings can pass through the fence openings, but good for gardens and small dogs.

Woven wire is a better option than welded wire because it is sturdier. The wire strands are woven or twisted together rather than welded. Two common kinds are field fencing and goat and sheep fencing. Suitable for cattle, goats, sheep, and pigs.

Knotted wire is similar to woven wire in that it isn't welded. Wire joins are individually wrapped or knotted. Available in either fixed knot or square knot styles, it is very sturdy and suitable for cattle, goats, sheep, and pigs.

Chicken wire

Poultry netting or hex-wire fencing is commonly referred to as "chicken wire." It comes in different widths with 1- or 2-inch openings and is available in various-gauge galvanized or PVC coated wire. The 6-foot height is recommenced for chickens, because they can easily hop or fly over 4-foot fences. Best suited for poultry.

No-climb (non-climb) is a type of horse fencing. The openings are too small for horses' hooves, so they can't step through the fence. It commonly comes in 48-inch or 60-inch heights. It's suitable for other kinds of livestock, but it's pricey.

Chain link is usually considered too expensive for livestock fencing, but if you already have it, there's no reason why you can't use it.

Panels

Panels are ready-made units that are used as both permanent and temporary fences, also for holding areas.

Stock panels (sometimes called "feedlot panels") are heavy-duty welded wire panels. Made of four-gauge wire, they come in 16-foot lengths of varying heights. Besides fencing, stock panels make good temporary reinforcement for welded wire fence in need of repair.

Cattle panels are the most common and least expensive. They are 50 to 52 inches high with openings large enough for chickens, goat kids, lambs, and baby pigs to pass through.

Hog panels are 34 inches tall with smaller openings. Best suited for pigs.

Goat panels are 48 inches in height and have smaller openings. Excellent for goats and sheep.

Horse panels have the smallest openings and are the most expensive. Height choices are 48 or 60 inches.

Corral panels are made of welded steel tubing and are usually used as corrals or holding areas. They are available in different heights and widths, but are best suited for large livestock such as cattle and horses. Goats, sheep, pigs, and poultry can get through these easily.

Corral panels

Electric Fencing

Electric fencing is classified as temporary (portable) or permanent. It is particularly useful for dividing pastures in a rotational grazing plan. Types include wire, netting, rope, twine, and tape. Animals must be trained to electric fencing, but once they learn they will get a zap when they touch it, they will keep clear. In general, one wire must be about nose-height of the animal you wish to contain. Ropes, twine, and tape are easier to see from a distance than wire. You will also need a solar or battery-powered fence charger.

* Cattle will need one to three wires for a cross fence, and four to six for boundaries.

* Goats and sheep will need two to five strands for a cross fence, six or seven for a boundary fence.

* Pigs will need three.

* Poultry need netting.

* Predator problem? Five and six strands are recommended to deter predators.

Electric fencing is often used in combination with any of the above permanent fencing types, typically as an offset hot wire to keep animals away from the fence. An electric wire on top will deter fence jumping. Electric fences must be checked periodically for branches, plant growth, or debris touching the wires.

Posts

Fence posts are classified as anchor and line posts, and bracing. They can be made of treated wood, steel, or fiberglass.

Anchor posts are treated wood posts used at corners and gates. Because they must support the tension of taut fencing they will be the heaviest, sturdiest posts, typically ranging from 6 to 8 inches in diameter. The ends are buried 3 to 4 feet deep. Three posts are needed for each corner and four are needed for each gate (two on each side). In loose, moist, or sandy soil, these should be set in concrete.

Line posts support the fencing between corners, gates, and bracing. Steel T-posts, fiberglass, or 2- to 3-inch treated wooden posts are common. These are equally spaced between anchor posts and bracing, and set about 2 feet into the ground.

Bracing is necessary to support long stretches of fence which would otherwise sag. For spans of fence longer than 165 feet, a brace will distribute the pull and stabilize the fencing wire. Depending on your soil, braces can be either singles (two brace posts connected with a horizontal cross-member and bracing wire) or for sandy soils, double braces (three brace posts, two cross-members, and bracing wire). Brace posts are usually treated wood with a 5- to 6-inch diameter.

GATES

Modern farm gates are either tube steel or mesh, and are available in widths from 4 to 16 feet. Make sure your gates are wide enough to enable you to transport materials, supplies, hay, and equipment to other areas of your property. An 8-foot gate easily accommodates our Chevy S-10 pickup truck and Ford 861 farm tractor.

For medium and small livestock, consider getting mesh gates. These are tube steel gates with stock paneling welded to them to prevent small animals from climbing through. If you want to build your own gates, however, then the sky's the limit in terms of materials and creativity.

Good latches or chains are a must. The bolted-on latches that come preinstalled on many gates can loosen if the gate receives a lot of pushing or ramming. There's nothing worse than finding your bucks chasing the does around after busting through such a gate. We like to use chains with bolt clips in addition to the latch.

ADDITIONAL SUPPLIES

For wire fences. In addition to the posts and wire, you will need:

* 9-gauge bracing wire
* auger or post hole digger

- fence stretcher
- fencing staples
- fencing tool for attaching wire to T-posts
- T-post clips
- T-post pounder

For electric fences. In addition to the wire, posts, and energizer (charger) you will need:

- clamps
- clips
- ground rod
- insulators
- tensioning tool
- wire

CHAPTER 4

FORAGE AND FEED

Livestock feeding has become extremely modernized over the years. On the one hand, this is convenient. We can simply load our pickup trucks with 50-pound bags of nutritionally complete packaged feed (called concentrates) and an occasional sack of minerals—what could be easier? From a preparedness perspective, however, this approach means I must purchase and store as much hay and feed as my preparedness plan prescribes. Or I can learn how to grow my own. But how do I take the feed bag ingredient list of roughage products, plant protein products, and grain by-products, and use that to formulate my own feeds? In this chapter, we'll take a look at feeding livestock from a self-reliance perspective.

PASTURE FOR FORAGING

"Forage" refers to the natural diet of plants that livestock eat as they graze. Forage includes grasses, legumes, and forbs. Grasses grow long-leaf blades and seeds on the end of a stalk. They provide energy and roughage. Legumes are nitrogen fixers such as clovers, peas, and beans. These provide protein. Forbs are broad-leaved herbs and flowering plants that provide vitamins and minerals. Unfortunately, soils today are so depleted and run-down that it is difficult for these plants to grow well and for animals to obtain the nutrition they need from free ranging alone. In this section, we'll look at pasture and how to improve it.

The best investment you can make in your homestead or farm is to build the soil. Healthy soils grow healthy plants, which means healthy livestock and healthy humans! Considering that so many health issues for plants, animals, and humans are based in nutrition, you can see how correcting soil problems will help prevent potential health problems. Soil building in a large pasture or paddock is more challenging than in a garden, however. There are two ways to build soil health: by correcting mineral imbalances and by adding organic matter. Healthy soil is maintained with plant diversity and rotational grazing.

Soil Minerals and Organic Matter

Most soils are depleted in organic matter and minerals. Or they have a mineral imbalance, which determines what can and can't grow. Your county cooperative extension can give you a basic soil analysis of pH, nitrogen, potassium, and phosphorous, but for a complete mineral analysis you will need to use a private laboratory. These will give you the most complete analysis, including pH, humus content, nitrogen, sulfate, phosphates, calcium, magnesium, potassium, sodium, and the trace minerals. See Chapter 4 Resources (page 210) for information for two soil-testing labs plus where to find organic soil amendments.

The goal for forage areas is to build topsoil, prevent erosion, and retain moisture by keeping the soil covered with plants. If your soils are compacted and depleted, however, you might want to consider a foundational plowing-in of manure, green manure, or imported topsoil along with your organic soil amendments.

Grazing animals will deposit manure and trample forage to add organic matter to the soil. When bare areas appear in our pasture, I seed them with an idea from Masanobu Fukuoka's *The One-Straw Revolution*. As I hand-broadcast the seeds, I lightly mulch them with old bedding from the goat barn or chicken coop. It covers the seed and decomposes to help build the soil in the no-till top-down manner.

Plant Diversity

A good pasture contains a wide variety of grasses, legumes, and forbs. When planting, aim for several dozen kinds of seeds, so you will always have something available for your livestock to eat. If one plant doesn't do well one year, something else will.

Plant diversity is also important for multispecies grazing. Farm animals vary in performance depending on the pasture. For example, sheep can have infertility problems if grazed on only clover. Cattle lose weight on tall fescue grass, while goats seem to tolerate it better.

Forage plants can be classified as warm- or cool-weather, also as annuals or perennials. Cool-weather forage is best suited for northern areas, but can be grown as winter pasture in warmer climates. Annual plants are good for variety and for spot-seeding bare areas, but perennials are important for permanent pasture.

None of the lists below are exhaustive.

Grasses

When Dan and I first bought our homestead, we just thought grass was grass. Not so! While some types are used for a variety of applications, others are better suited for specific purposes.

Lawn versus pasture grass. Some grasses are used for both lawn and pasture, such as Bahia, Bermuda, Bluegrass, and fescue. For pasture or hay growing, avoid types that are described as "low-growing." These are better suited for lawns.

Turf versus pasture grass. Turf grasses offer dense cover with a thick mat of roots. They are good for golf courses, sports fields, and low-maintenance monoculture pastures. If your goal is forage diversity, however, they will choke out other plants. Examples are Bahia, Bermuda, Bluegrass, and fescue.

Native versus commercial grasses. Commercial grasses are the ones you'll commonly find recommended for pasture, for example, Bahia, Bermuda, fescue, orchard grass, and timothy. Native grasses, on the other hand, are natural grasses that grow without cultivation. Examples include bluestems, buffalo grass, Indian grass, gama grass,

Buffalo grass

and switchgrass. You'll need to do some research to determine which ones are native to your area, but it's a worthwhile study. They can be difficult to establish, but are more drought, frost, flood, and disease tolerant than many of the commercial varieties. They require no fertilizer but have excellent nutritional value. In addition to forage and hay, native grasses are excellent for erosion control, biomass, riparian buffer strips, and wildlife habitat.

Invasive grasses. Invasive species are those that take over and dominate where they are planted. They can be native or non-native. Bermuda grass is a commercial grass that is highly invasive, spreading by both roots and seeds. Many native grasses are also considered invasive, and thus are illegal to plant in some places. Check with your state agriculture department or county cooperative extension agent for information specific to your area.

All the plants in the charts below are commonly used for pasture and can be purchased from a farm seed supplier. Some can be purchased in seed mixes. I recommend that you do your homework before you buy. For example, sorghum, Sudan grass, and Johnsongrass are highly prized grasses because of their drought resistance but should not be grazed after a frost, because freezing changes their chemical composition.

Also see Minerals and Vitamins on page 87.

OVERVIEW OF GRASSES

	ANNUALS	PERENNIALS (* INDICATES NATIVE GRASS)
WARM WEATHER	Egyptian wheat	Bahia grass
	millet	Bermuda grass
	sorghum	bluestem*
	Sudan	Chufa
		Dallis grass
		Eastern gama grass*
		Indian grass*
		Johnsongrass
		switchgrass
COOL WEATHER	annual ryegrass	bromegrass
	barley	fescue (novel endophyte)
	oats	Kentucky bluegrass
	rye grain	orchard grass
	triticale	perennial ryegrass
	wheat	timothy

OVERVIEW OF LEGUMES

	ANNUALS	PERENNIALS
WARM WEATHER	annual lespedeza	alfalfa
	cowpeas	birdsfoot trefoil
	partridge pea	sericea lespedeza
COOL WEATHER	winter peas	clover
	vetch	sainfoin

OVERVIEW OF FORBS

	ANNUALS	PERENNIALS
WARM WEATHER	buckwheat	chicory
	sunflower	comfrey
		coneflower
		oregano
		plantain
		small burnet
		thyme
		small burnet
COOL WEATHER	collards	small burnet
	kale	fescue (novel endophyte)
	mustard	Kentucky bluegrass
	radish	orchard grass
	rape	perennial ryegrass
	sugar beets	timothy
	turnips	

Kudzu

Kudzu is a legume you may see mentioned for livestock. It's highly invasive so I don't recommend planting it. However, if you've already got it growing, use it! It's considered equal in nutrition to alfalfa and can be fed fresh or dried for a nutritious hay.

ROTATIONAL GRAZING

This is a widely recommended method for parasite control in grazing animals. Parasite eggs are deposited on the ground through manure. After several days, they hatch and the larvae begin to climb pasture plants, where there are ingested by the same animals and repeat their life cycle. If you remove grazers from the pasture for a period of time, parasite larvae can't find a new host and begin to die off. This requires at least two pasture areas. Recommended time for rest varies from 21 to 60 days, with no specific data regarding how long parasite larvae and especially eggs can survive without a host.

The other benefit of rotational grazing is that plants have time to rest and grow again after being grazed. All animals will eat what they like best first, and if allowed to overgraze their favorites, they can eventually kill them, leaving the less-palatable plants to dominate the pasture. Pastured pigs will begin to root. This is useful if you need some tilling done, but to maintain good-quality forage, plan to rotate your livestock when forage is grazed down to 3 to 4 inches in height.

Poultry is often allowed to free range, but if you have problems with predators or need to keep them off of newly seeded areas, portable pens such as chicken tractors are a good solution. These also work well for pasturing rabbits. These pens contain a coop or hutch for shelter, waterers, and nest boxes for laying hens. One precaution for rabbits is that they tend to dig and will indeed dig their way to freedom. The solution for that comes from Daniel Salatin at Polyface Farms. His hare pens have slatted bottoms. Narrow slats with several inches in between allow rabbits to access pasture forage but not dig out and escape.

In general, rotational grazing is easiest to manage if your grazing areas are all accessible from your barn. A corral or holding area is fenced off from the barn, and you can direct animals to the various pastures by simply opening a gate.

Intensive Rotational Grazing

This is a land-management system based on the natural grazing patterns of migratory herds of animals. It was developed by Allan Savory for reclaiming desertified grasslands in Zimbabwe. It is more commonly known in the US as "mob grazing."

Pastures are divided into paddocks large enough for livestock to eat down to 3 or 4 inches in height within one to four days. Then they are moved to the next paddock. They leave behind their manure in a trampled paddock, which is allowed to rest. During this recovery time, soil organisms feed on the manure and trampled plants, building the soil while continuing to grow diverse plant life.

Intensive rotational grazing is easiest when the livestock can simply be moved from one paddock to the next. That means it's best suited for livestock that spend the night in the field. Considerations here are water availability in every paddock, plus protection against predators, especially for smaller animals such as sheep and goats.

Multispecies Grazing

Diversity is always the natural pattern, and allowing several species of livestock to graze the same pasture follows this pattern. The result is a more productive use of the land. The most common use of this system is cattle with small ruminants—goats and sheep. Of grasses, forbs, and shrubs, cattle distinctly prefer grasses. Sheep like both grass and forbs, and goats prefer forbs and shrubs. Grazing these species together means there is minimal competition for forage while better utilizing it. In fact, goats and sheep offer good weed control for plants that cattle won't eat. Goats in particular are used to control otherwise undesirable shrubs and vines: multiflora roses, blackberry brambles, poison ivy, and kudzu, for example. Another benefit is that cows have different internal parasites than the small ruminants, so grazing them together provides some measure of parasite control.

Chickens and turkeys work well with this mix, because they scratch and scatter manure, plus eat seeds, insects, and grubs. Ducks don't scratch; rather, they use their bills to shovel through the soil in search of things to eat. However, ducks make it challenging to keep drinking water clean. They will swim in drinking water or use it to clean their bills, leaving it too dirty for ruminants to drink.

Pigs love pasture but also tend to root. Use them in wooded areas where goats can browse and pigs can root. Keep the goats' drinking water higher than the pigs can reach. Pig snouts leave water very dirty, which goats won't drink. If they can, pigs will knock over the water buckets to make mud.

There are other precautions to heed. Some animals will bully others, so those aren't good individuals for this system. Species differ in mineral needs as well. Sheep, for example, are more sensitive to copper, while goats tend to be copper deficient. Care must be taken to meet both of their needs.

UTILIZING UNFENCED AREAS

If you have access to unfenced grassy, forage, or browse areas, you can let your livestock take advantage with temporary fencing or by tethering.

Temporary electric fencing. We have several areas around our homestead that are not part of our pasture and become overgrown with shrubs and vines. I use electric netting and a solar fence charger to temporarily fence these off and allow the chickens, goats, and pigs to eat them down. Electric netting works best for poultry; otherwise, electric wires can be used, as long as the animals have been trained to them.

Tethering. Tethering is another way to expand forage options. It was once common practice but is not well known today. Animals can get tangled up, however, so there are some things to consider before attempting to tether your milk cow.

* Tethering is best suited for ruminants six months of age or older.

* The animal must be trained to both lead and tether.

* The tether must be able to swivel around its anchor point.

* The area must be free of poisonous plants and trash. No, goats don't really eat tin cans, but some have been known to ingest plastic. Cows can and will ingest small bits of metal debris. This

detrimental condition is referred to as "hardware disease" and requires veterinary assistance.

* Success depends on the individual's personality. A high-strung animal can panic if it becomes tangled.

* A good length for a tether is 20 feet.

* Chain or polyrope are commonly used for tethers.

* Shade and water should be available.

* Tethered animals must be checked on frequently. Do not leave an animal tethered if you leave the farm.

* Change the location as needed.

Tethering requires some work and maintenance, but for unfenced areas around the barn or house, it can offer grass and weed trimming as well as more grazing for your livestock.

UTILIZING BROWSE

"Browse" refers to the woody shrubs, vines, sapling trees, and other plants preferred by deer, goats, and some sheep. Given a choice, goats will always prefer browse to pasture, which is why they are often used for brush control. Browse is more difficult to maintain, however, because it is slower growing. Following are two techniques for offering browse.

Permaculture hedgerows. Hedgerows between pastures act as windbreaks and shelter for wildlife. Dan and I use permaculture hedgerows to offer additional forage for our goats. Ours are planted between two rows of cattle panels and include fruit and nut trees as well as bushes, herbs, and other tasty ground cover. The goats can eat some of the forage through the cattle panels, but can't eat it down and eradicate it.

If your pastures are more than 200 yards from woods or brush, consider adding hedgerows. They will offer welcome cover for insect-eating birds, plus add forage diversity for your small ruminants.

Shepherding. I love taking my goats for walks in our woods. They love it too, and when I say, "Let's go for a walk," the girls will run to the gate. They love the browse in the woods, but also, my neighbor lets me walk them in his back field. It's overrun with blackberry and kudzu, and he doesn't mind a measure of goat control! This works for me because my goats know me well, trust me, and are willing to follow me.

The key to successful shepherding is being able to control your animals. This can be accomplished either through trust, as with my few goats, or with a herding dog who knows its business. Allowing livestock to run free with no measure of control is irresponsible. To shepherd (to tend, guard, herd, lead, or drive), however, may be an option for you.

Shepherding

PURCHASING HAY

Hay is pasture forage that has been dried and stored for times when livestock can't graze. This can be because of heavy snowfall, heavy rain, dormant pasture, or times of confinement such as birthing. For ruminants, hay is important for healthy digestion and nutrient assimilation. Even though many of us have a goal to produce all or some of our own hay, most of us buy hay when we first get livestock. First, I'll discuss some things to know about buying hay, and then I'll give you some information on growing your own.

Hay is described in several ways. I addressed bale shapes and sizes in Chapter 3, Barns, Shelters, and Fences, so here are a few other ways you may see hay described when purchasing.

By contents: Hay is usually advertised by the kind of forage it contains: Bermuda grass, fescue, alfalfa, mixed grass, or perhaps a grass and legume mix such as orchard grass and clover.

By quality: Often hay is described as either horse- or cow-quality. These aren't official classifications, however, and their definition may vary depending on where you live.

* Horse quality is generally the better-quality pure grass hay. It is often fertilized, sprayed, and contains no weeds.

* Cow quality is generally weedier hay, unless you live in dairy country. Then it can mean a good-quality alfalfa hay. Alfalfa is good for milk cows but considered too rich for beef cattle, so be sure to ask what the seller means by "cow quality."

* Goat-quality is rarely used, but from what I've seen, it is usually "hay" baled from a field of dead weeds. Unfortunately, too many people believe that goats will eat anything, including poor-quality hay. In truth, goats are very picky eaters and will reject hay like that.

By cutting: Depending on what part of the country you are in, up to three cuttings may be made from one stand. Experienced livestock folks will ask which cutting the hay is if this isn't advertised.

* First cutting hay is made in the late spring and the grasses typically have more stems and fewer leaves. It will have a higher percentage of grasses than legumes, which grow more slowly. It's usually higher in fiber and carbohydrates than protein.

- Second cutting is harvested in mid-summer. It is leafier with fewer stems. It is lower in sugars because of faster growth, but rich in other nutrients such as proteins if it contains early legumes.

- Third cutting is harvested in late summer or early fall. It usually contains more of the slow-growing legumes and is rich in nutrients.

Other purchasing considerations: Be sure to examine the bales before you buy them. Good hay should be dry but green and not contain seed heads. It should also not contain noxious weeds such as horse nettle. Never buy or feed moldy hay. Some kinds of mold can cause serious problems for livestock. Ask these questions if the ad doesn't specifically mention these things:

- What year was it cut?

- Has it been stored in the field or in a barn? Hay that has been allowed to sit outdoors will be lower quality than barn-kept hay.

- Has it been sprayed with herbicides? Ask if the ad doesn't tell you and that's important to you.

GROWING HAY

On our homestead, we try to grow and harvest as much of our own hay as possible. In our pasture areas, we cut forage for hay when the goats can't keep up with it. Also, we have set aside a few small unfenced areas specifically for growing hay. Any seed that is used for pasture can be used for hay. I hand-broadcast our seed because the handheld and push-seed spreaders are better suited for lawn seed than the mix I plant. If you have a tractor and grain drill, you can plant more quickly with less seed.

We generally have mild winters and can grow both warm- and cool-weather forage for hay. Wheat and oats can be cut before they go to seed, or when the seed is in the "milk stage" (i.e., before it has completely dried). Animals love this hay with grain combo.

Harvesting Hay

Hay is most nutritious if cut before going to seed. Some grasses, such as Sudan grass, forage sorghum, millet, and native grasses grow up to 5 feet or more in height and develop inedible cane-like stalks. We cut these at knee height. Harvest depends on cooperative weather, of course, so plan for enough days for complete drying before raking up.

As with all things on our homestead, we have both a high-tech and a low-tech tool for the job. Our high-tech haying tool is a walk-behind sickle mower. Similar to a lawn mower, it has a vibrating sickle bar for cutting hay. Its disadvantages are that it's expensive to buy, requires gasoline to run, and is noisy. It's mechanical, so it requires more maintenance than a hand tool. But it is a time-saver. If you have many acres of hay to cut, a sickle bar will be a handy attachment for your tractor during haying. For low-tech hay cutting, we manually scythe our hay. It takes more time, but it's quieter, easier to maintain, and will always be there even if gasoline is not.

Of scythes, there are two types: American and European (Austrian). A scythe has two parts: the scythe (blade) and the snath (handle). A properly fitted scythe allows you to stand straight, not hunch. The cutting movement is rhythmic and done from the shoulders without twisting the lower back.

Dan has both types and prefers the European scythe, because European snaths come in a choice of lengths with adjustable hand grips and a choice of blades.

Drying Hay

Hay is cut while leafy and green and dried in the field. Depending on the humidity, it must be turned one or more times to loosen it and dry the underside. We turn ours by hand with a garden rake, although wooden hay rakes are also available. If you have too much to do by hand, consider getting a tractor attachment called a "tedder" to turn the hay for you.

Hay must be completely dry before baling and storing. Like all organic matter, it contains bacteria, which produce heat as the plant material decomposes. If hay is still green when baled or stacked, it will generate heat as it decomposes and will work its way into compost.

Raking hay

This can also result in spontaneous combustion (seriously!), so that the hay actually catches fire.

Other Sources for Hay

While I grow and harvest much of our hay, I also harvest from several other sources:

Fence lines: I use a hand sickle to harvest grasses, weeds, and legumes along our fence lines where the scythe or sickle mower can't get. These are dried and tossed onto the hay pile.

Garden and orchard: Again, I use my hand sickle to trim whatever areas need them, such as overgrown garden beds or around the bases of fruit and nut bushes and trees.

Kudzu: I live where kudzu can be a problem. However, it is an excellent feed for livestock, both fresh and dried. Other problem vines can be added as well, such as honeysuckle and morning glory. For anything else, please read What's Poisonous? What's Not? on page 80.

Storing Hay

If you don't have a baler, not to worry! We don't and store our harvested hay in piles. Wood is the best surface on which to store hay, either in a structure or on a wood platform in a hoop house. Concrete sweats and the ground wicks moisture, so these work best if a platform, pallet, or bed of branches can provide a base. For more information on hay storage, see page 49.

Other Considerations

Hay yield per acre. Production can range from 1.5 to 7 or so tons per acre depending on type of hay, soil fertility, and number of cuttings.

Estimating feeding needs. Calculations are usually made based on animal body weight. Here are some helpful feeding guidelines:

HAY FEEDING NEEDS

ANIMAL	CALCULATION	DAILY AMOUNT	MONTHLY AMOUNT
COW	2% of body weight	25 pounds per cow	1 ton per cow
GOAT	3% of body weight	4 pounds per goat	150 pounds per goat
SHEEP	4% of body weight	5 pounds per sheep	225 pounds per sheep
PIG	1% of body weight	2 pounds per pig	55 pounds per pig
RABBIT	5% of body weight	½ pound per rabbit	14 pounds per rabbit

These are generalized estimates and amounts may vary depending on whom you ask, but this will give you a starting point from which to work.

USING FEED

Preppers have two options when it comes to animal feeds: Stock up on packaged feeds or grow your own. Purchased grain or grain-based pellets (concentrates) are certainly the most convenient way to feed livestock, but homesteaders and preppers usually aspire to feed their animals from their land. Animal nutrition and mixing your own feed rations, however, can be a very complex subject, one that is beyond the scope of this handbook, so please consider the following information as an introduction to the subject. After you read through this section, check Resources for information to help you achieve your personal feed goals.

To make the best choices for feeding your livestock, I think it's important to understand how their digestive systems work. The best feeds for any species are those it was designed to eat.

Monogastric animals. These are animals with one stomach. Digestive acids and enzymes break down foods into various nutrients that are absorbed to some degree in the stomach, but primarily in the intestines. This type of digestion is well-suited for concentrates such as grains as well as pasture. Concentrates are high in energy (carbohydrates) but low in fiber. Monogastrics require true protein, i.e. amino acids, in their diets. Pigs are omnivorous examples of animals with monogastric digestive systems.

Avian digestion. Poultry have a single stomach plus a crop and a gizzard. The gizzard takes the place of teeth. Birds eat bits of gravel, which grind grains into smaller pieces. The crop predigests grains and seeds, using the enzyme amylase to break starches into easily absorbed sugars. In addition to grasses, bugs, worms, grubs, and other tidbits, grains and seeds are a good choice for your poultry.

Ruminants. Ruminants like cows, goats, and sheep have four stomachs that utilize fermentation to extract nutrients. Their digestive systems are best suited for roughages, particularly high-cellulose forage plants and hay. In addition to enzymes, ruminants have digestive microbes, which are able to extract nutrients such as nitrogen from roughage and utilize it to make protein. During ruminal fermentation, volatile fatty acids are produced. These in turn provide energy—enough, in fact, to keep the animal warm during winter.

Slow changes in diet are advised for ruminants to allow gut microbes to adjust. Grains can be a problem because grain ferments as it sits in the rumen and increases its acidity. See Acidosis on page 170 for more information. Roughage in the form of forage and long-stemmed hay is the best diet for ruminants. Goats, cattle, sheep, and deer are examples.

Pseudo-ruminant. These animals have three-chambered stomachs and can also utilize large amounts of roughage. Llamas, alpacas, and rabbits are pseudo-ruminants. Horses are sometimes included in this category because, although they are monogastric, they have an enlarged cecum, which allows for what is called "hind-gut fermentation" of pasture and hay. Pseudo-ruminants can digest concentrates, but high-fiber, low-starch diets are usually recommended for optimal health.

What all this means is that you don't have to grow several acres' worth of grain to replace store-bought feed pellets. This is especially true for ruminants and pseudo-ruminants; put your land into high-quality forage rather than grain. Grain can be grown on a much smaller scale while you focus on feed alternatives.

What are those alternatives? The following lists will give you some ideas.

USING GRAIN

Even though you won't need acres and acres of grain, you may still want to grow it. Grain provides energy (carbohydrates) and is easy to grow. The harder part is the harvesting and processing (removing the grain from the seed heads). However, for most livestock, processing doesn't have to be as extensive as you might think.

Cereal grains. Cereal grains such as wheat, oats, and barley require minimal processing except for pigs. Pigs will prefer their grain threshed and winnowed. Poultry, on the other hand, instinctively know to peck the grains from the whole heads. For ruminants and rabbits, cereal grains can be fed as whole plants. Cut for hay after seed heads have formed but while the plant is still leafy. This is my preferred way to feed grain to my goats. It minimizes the amount of starch while providing the roughage necessary to help them properly digest it. Chaff from cereal grains can be fed to ruminants too.

Corn. This is one of the easiest grains to process, although for pigs that isn't necessary. Toss a few ears of corn to a pig, and it will readily remove every kernel from the cob. Chickens do better if the corn has been shelled. Corn is deficient in lysine, however, so if you feed a lot of corn, also feed a legume to balance the amino acids. Corn leaves are relished by ruminants. Ground corn cobs and stalks can be added to feed for extra carbohydrates.

Cracked grains. Does grain need to be cracked before feeding? Grain is cracked for poultry because of size. It is cracked for larger livestock to make it more digestible. Whole grains often pass through the animal whole, which then begs the question addressed before: Are grains the best feed for your livestock?

I feed all grains whole, including corn. I grow a small-kerneled, open-pollinated variety called Trucker's Favorite. Its grains are small enough that it doesn't require the additional time and equipment to crack. If you want to crack your grain, you can use a home grain mill adjusted to the coarse grind. On a large scale, you will need a hammer mill. See Build Your Own Hammer Mill in Chapter 4 Resources (page 210) for more information.

Exotic grains. Amaranth and milo (grain sorghum) are commonly grown for livestock. They are easy to grow and develop large heads of small seeds (the grain) that are easy to harvest. For chickens, whole seed heads can be tossed into the yard. For ruminants, whole dried heads can be chopped and fed, as can the leaves, stalks, and stems. Quinoa is also sometimes mentioned as livestock feed; however, it contains saponins, which are a concern and so must be removed prior to using it as feed. Quinoa leaves, however, are good for ruminants.

Sprouted grains. This is an excellent way to stretch your grain budget. People who feed sprouted grains report a 50 percent reduction in the amount of grain they have to feed and I have experienced the same. Sprouting trays work best for large amounts. They are ready to feed when growth is about a quarter of an inch.

Fermented grains. Lacto-fermentation of grain is a good option for monogastric livestock such as pigs, as well as poultry. As with sauerkraut or kombucha, fermented grain contains more vitamins and minerals than unfermented, plus probiotics. Making it is simple: Pour grain into a bucket and cover with water. Depending on air temperature, it will begin to bubble in one to three days. That's when it's ready to feed. We scoop it out into a colander and let it drain back into the bucket. The white film that forms on top is yeast, not mold. It can be skimmed and discarded if you wish. Our chickens and ducks love fermented grain. Just make sure the grain stays covered with liquid, or it will become moldy. Discard moldy grain.

Pasture grass seeds. These are also grain, but available on the stalk in the pasture. Poultry will eat the seeds right off the plants, and goats will eat the entire seed head.

USING LEGUMES

Legumes add protein to the diet, both as pasture plants and hay. Some legume seeds and peas make good feed as well. Pastured herbivores will consume much of their protein as legumes. Omnivores will include insects, larvae, and earthworms as sources of protein in their diet. With a diverse, healthy pasture, the need for additional protein supplements will be minimal.

Legumes for feed mixes include the following possibilities:

* Field peas are easy to grow, are roughly 23 percent protein, and can be fed as whole plants, as hay, in the pod, or processed. Some of the small varieties do not need to be cracked for poultry.

* Lentils are another possibility, with 26 percent protein. They can be fed as whole plants or like grain.

* Beans such as soy, navy, broad, or other dried beans are not recommended as they contain digestive inhibitors that can cause nutritional problems for livestock. Processing of beans for feed also requires heat treatment that isn't practical on a small scale.

Seeds

Seeds also provide protein, plus vitamin E and omega fatty acids. They are rich, so small amounts are best.

* Sunflower seeds, particularly black oil sunflower seeds, can be fed in the shell. They provide protein, energy, selenium, and vitamin E. For ruminants, the entire seed head can be chopped and fed.

* Sesame seeds are rich in B vitamins, calcium, copper, magnesium, and zinc.

* Flaxseeds provide protein, energy from the oil, vitamin E, and omega fatty acids. They can be fed in the hull.

MAKING YOUR OWN FEED RATIONS

In the introduction, I mentioned pondering over the ingredients listed on a feed bag label and wondering how I could make my own feeds. Grains and legumes are certainly the primary ingredients in any pelleted feed, but what about the other things mentioned, such as roughage, forage, and grain by-products? What are they and are they necessary? Here's a rundown of what you'll typically see listed on a feed bag and what that means.

Grain products: Corn, wheat, oats, barley, etc.

Plant protein products: Soy meal, cottonseed meal, linseed meal, yeast, etc.

Animal protein products: Hydrolyzed poultry feathers, blood meal, fish meal, meat meal, dried whey, dried milk, etc.

Roughage products: Various hulls and pulps including cottonseed, grain, and peanut hulls; beet and dried apple pulp, etc.

Forage products: Basically hay meal, including both legume hay (alfalfa, lespedeza, etc.) and grass hay (Bermuda, timothy, etc.)

Processed grain by-products: Dried brewers and distillers grains, corn gluten, wheat millings, bran (rice, wheat, etc.)

In addition, you will see a number of vitamins and minerals listed on the label.

Commercial feeds, then, are grain, legumes, and filler, usually with molasses as a binder to hold the pellets together. Understanding that makes it easier to make my own feeds with the ingredients of my choosing. What can I use for fillers? Basically any palatable thing that I can dry and chop: leaves and stalks from various plants (corn, sorghum, amaranth, and Jerusalem artichoke), whole sunflower seed heads, corn cobs, hulls from wheat winnowing, etc. I use a small-scale chipper/shredder to chop these, and catch them in a small drum.

How do I know that this homemade feed is meeting our critters' nutritional needs? Good question. One way is to have a nutrient analysis done on your feed mix. These are available through most state agricultural offices. Check with your county cooperative extension office for more information.

If I know the crude protein content of each of the ingredients going into my feed mix, I can use a formula called the Pearson Square to calculate how many of each I will need for a specific percentage of protein. This formula was originally developed to standardize the amounts of fat and protein in commercially produced milk. Since then, it has been used for making wine, fruit juice blends, cheese, and animal feed. It can be used for any animal and any nutrient, although protein is probably the most common. See Chapter 4 Resources on page 210 for where to find more information.

WHAT'S POISONOUS? WHAT'S NOT?

Garden produce and foraged wild foods usually raise the question of what is safe to feed livestock. It's a valid question, and if you've done much research on this topic, you have likely noticed that the various lists sometimes contradict one another. Even the livestock experts don't always agree, and this is true of individual testimony as well. Some folks will say something killed their goat, others may say their goats eat it all the time.

In some cases, it may be only part of the plant that causes problems. Most gardeners know that the fruit of the tomato plant is edible, but the leaves and stems are toxic. Some plants may be toxic in certain conditions but not others. Johnson and Sudan grasses, for example, are only toxic after a frost or a drought. At other times, they are fine. Wild cherry and chokecherry leaves contain cyanide, but only when wilted, not fresh. Some things are okay in limited quantities, such as brassicas, but in large quantities, they can interfere with the thyroid's uptake of iodine. Azalea and rhododendron, on the other hand, are never fine. They cause acute poisoning every time and can lead to death.

In this section, I'll give you guidelines for feeding garden and foraged plants to your animals, and provide some lists of possibilities. Be sure to check Resources to learn where to find more detailed lists and databases of poisonous and edible plants. And remember that any changes of diet should be slow to allow digestive systems to adapt.

I do recommend that you add good plant identification books to your homestead library. These need to be specific for plants grown in your area and include scientific names. Common names for plants can vary by location, so when you look them up on the lists, verify the scientific name for accurate identification.

You should also follow these guidelines when choosing produce and foraged foods.

❊ Cross-reference several lists. If something appears on all the poisonous plants lists I look at, then I know it is definitely something to avoid.

❊ Do not assume animals will only eat edible plants. Often you will read that animals know instinctively not to eat things that will harm them. While that may be generally true, don't assume it's an absolute truth. A starving animal will eat anything available, including poisonous plants. This can be true with nutrient deficiencies as well.

❊ Keep your forage areas healthy and as diverse as possible. I have a few poisonous plants that I am constantly battling with, such as horse nettle. It is very difficult to eradicate, but with plenty of tastier plants on offer, my goats ignore it.

❊ For ruminants and rabbits, provide plenty of free-choice hay. The digestion of long-stemmed roughage will dilute the effect of potential toxins they might ingest.

❊ Never feed moldy hay or feeds. Molds often produce toxins that can cause problems, including death.

❊ Include as much variety in your animals' diets as possible, and always keep good-quality hay on offer.

❊ When in doubt, don't.

Garden Produce

Now on to something more positive—things livestock *can* safely eat! The following list is by no means comprehensive, but it includes many things that my critters enjoy.

In general, root crops, rinds, and peels can be fed whole to chickens, pigs, rabbits, and cattle. In fact, it gives them something to do and slows down competitive speed eating. Goats prefer their feeds chopped into small pieces.

- amaranth, leaves and seed heads
- apples, leaves and fruit, including cores
- basil
- beans, pods and plants
- beets, roots and leaves
- blueberries, berries, leaves, and twigs
- broccoli
- broom corn, leaves and seeds
- cabbage
- cantaloupe, fruit, seeds, and rind
- carrots, roots and leaves
- celery
- chicory leaves
- citrus fruits (I have dwarf plants in pots)
- collard greens
- comfrey leaves and flower stalks
- corn, husks, silk, and leaves
- cowpeas, pods and plants
- cucumber fruits
- dill
- figs, fruit and leaves
- flax seed in the pod
- garlic, whole plant
- grapefruit rind
- horseradish leaves
- Jerusalem artichokes, leaves and tubers
- kale
- mangels, roots and leaves
- melons, fruit, seeds, and rind
- mint
- mulberry, leaves
- mustard greens
- okra, pods and leaves
- oregano
- parsley
- parsnips, roots and leaves
- pear, leaves and fruit, including cores
- peas, green, pods and vines
- plum, leaves and fruit

- potatoes, tubers (can feed raw)
- pumpkin, seeds, pulp, and rind
- radish, roots and leaves
- raspberry, leaves, vines, and berries
- rosemary
- roses, flowers, leaves, vines, and hips
- sorghum, leaves and seeds
- squash, summer and winter, fruits, rinds, and seeds
- strawberry, fruit and leaves
- sugar beet, roots and leaves
- sunflowers, seeds and heads
- sweet potatoes, tubers and vines
- Swiss chard, leaves
- thyme
- tomatoes, fruits only
- turnips, roots and leaves
- yarrow

Wild Foods

When seeking out wild foods, 1) be sure to make proper identification of all plants and check the edibility for any you question and 2) don't gather from roadsides or areas that might have been sprayed with herbicides or pesticides.

- acorns, white oak
- althea (hardy hibiscus)
- blackberry, leaves, vines, and berries
- cedar, leafy branches
- chickweed
- cleavers
- dandelion, leaves
- daylily, flowers and leaves
- English ivy
- honeysuckle vines, leaves, and flowers
- kudzu vines
- Ligustrum, leaves and branches
- magnolia, leafy branches
- morning glory
- oak leaves

- pecan (hickory) leaves
- plantain leaves
- pine, leafy branches
- poison ivy
- raspberry, leaves, vines, and berries
- roses, leaves, vines, flowers, hips
- vetch

Stover

Stover is the dried stalks and leaves of various plants fed to livestock after the grain has been harvested. Possibilities include corn, sunflower, sorghum, and Jerusalem artichoke stalks. The only precaution is to only feed dried stalks with no mold.

Hydroponic Fodder

This is an exceptionally useful feed for urban and suburban chicken and rabbit keeping. Grain is sprouted in trays, rinsed daily, and allowed to grow into new grass. Since no dirt is involved, the mat of dense roots and grass is simply broken into chunks and fed as is.

This system does require some equipment: trays, a tray rack, and a way to catch water drainage. Also, it requires some temperature control (low 60s °F/mid to upper teens °C). It takes about eight days to produce, but is said to cut grain bills by 50 to 75 percent. One pound of grain yields approximately 4 to 6 pounds of fodder.

See Chapter 4 Resources on page 210 for more information.

Silage (Ensilage)

Silage is forage that has been lacto-fermented as a means of preservation. Plants are harvested while they are green and succulent and allowed to ferment anaerobically, much like sauerkraut. Chaffhaye is a popular brand of alfalfa silage (also called haylage). On large farms silos are usually used for the process, but ensiling can be done on a small scale in sealed plastic bags or 55-gallon drums.

The advantages are preservation of fresh forage plus increased nutrition and the addition of probiotics. However, as with all lacto-fermentation there is something of an art to it. The process must be done without oxygen, because oxygen fosters the growth of mold. It requires a means to chop the forage into small sizes, plus a working and storage area. Moisture, temperature, and fermenting gases must be monitored. All of that is extra work, but depending on your situation, it may be a good option. See Chapter 4 Resources on page 210 for more information.

More Options for Poultry

We like to let our poultry free range the pasture as much as possible. Sometimes they can't; for example, any time I've seeded or mulched pasture areas. For times when they need to stay in their yard, we have several options for homegrown feed. See also the discussion on chicken tractors on page 64, and hydroponic fodder, discussed above.

Compost bins. We keep our compost piles in the chicken yard. We use a three-bin system: one for adding to, one for working compost, and one for finished compost. The chickens have access to all three, but only eat from the adding and working piles. They scratch for the tidbits they want and help turn the leftovers into compost.

Compost piles for chickens still require some turning, because they are primarily surface scratchers. By turning frequently to expose weed seeds and sprouts, our chickens find more to eat and our compost is more weed and seed free than it used to be.

Composting worms. Some gardeners keep worm bins to make excellent garden fertilizer from kitchen scraps called castings. Like all other living things, compost worms reproduce themselves, which also makes the surplus a viable source of homegrown protein for poultry. Any time your worm bed looks crowded, toss a few handfuls into the poultry yard.

Grazing frames. Grazing frames are raised garden beds that are covered with hardware cloth. Grazing plants such as wheat or oats are grown in these beds specifically for poultry. Once the grasses grow several inches above the bed, the birds are allowed to graze. The hardware cloth is study enough for them to stand on, but protects the grass from being overgrazed. These can be rotated, so that chickens have continual access to fresh grasses.

Considerations for Rabbits

I mentioned ways to pasture rabbits earlier in this chapter (see Intensive Rotational Grazing on page 64). Most people who pasture rabbits still offer supplemental foods to their rabbits in addition to hay. The most commonly recommended diet for rabbits is commercial rabbit feed. This diet is so widely accepted that folks often forget that rabbits lived for millennia without store-bought pellets! Organic pellets are available, but what if you want to use homegrown feeds instead?

The problem with switching from those pellets to a natural diet is that sudden changes can wreak digestive havoc. If your rabbits are used to commercial rabbit feed, make very slow changes in what you feed them. A natural diet recommended by the House Rabbit Society (per two pounds of rabbit body weight) is:

* 1 cup fresh greens

* 1 tablespoon other fresh vegetables

* 1 teaspoon fruit

The above can be fed whole, as rabbits love to gnaw. You must also feed free-choice, good-quality grass hay, such as timothy. (Free-choice means that animals have free access and can eat as much as they want.)

High-calcium foods such as alfalfa are usually advised against, because commercial rabbit feeds contain quite a bit of alfalfa. If you are feeding a grass hay or greens-based diet, however, alfalfa (fresh or as hay) will add protein to the diet. Offer alfalfa, along with other high-calcium greens such as collards, kale, and turnip greens in moderation, because while rabbits need some calcium, too much can cause bladder and urinary tract problems.

Grains, seeds, and fruit can cause obesity and should be fed sparingly. Legumes and nuts are not recommended. I've included links to extensive rabbit diet lists in Resources, but as with other lists, opinions of what's safe and what isn't varies quite a bit. Always add new foods slowly and in small amounts. If the rabbit develops diarrhea or seems unwell, discontinue that particular food. Like people, individual rabbits can have different tolerances for various foods.

MINERALS AND VITAMINS

Minerals and vitamins are key to good health in all living things. Livestock get most of these from foraging, but deficiencies can occur if they are fed corn- and soy-based feeds or if pasture and hay are grown in mineral-deficient soils. In some areas, regional soils have specific mineral deficiencies such as copper and selenium. Your best course of action is to obtain a detailed soil analysis and then remineralize your soil according to the soil report recommendations. Second best is to offer these minerals as a free-choice supplement.

Mineral blocks work best for cattle, who get what they need by licking the block. Rabbit block minerals come in spools which are attached to their cages. Loose minerals are a better choice for goats and sheep. These are fed free choice so the animals can help themselves as needed. One note of precaution—goats require more copper than sheep, which creates a logistic challenge for the mineral feeder if these species are housed together. Pigs are sometimes offered loose or block minerals, especially if they are confined or primarily on packaged feeds. Some people offer free-choice kelp to their poultry.

Another option for meeting vitamin and mineral needs is to grow your own. Nutrient-rich plants can be grown, harvested, chopped, and added to feed either fresh or dried.

Also see Nutritional Balance on page 166 for more information on mineral and vitamin deficiencies.

Vitamins

A and Beta-Carotene: basil, butternut squash, cantaloupe, carrots, collard greens, dandelion greens, dill, grape leaves, kale, marjoram, mustard greens, oregano, parsley, spinach, sweet potatoes, thyme, turnip greens

B1 (Thiamin): kudzu, rosemary, sage, sesame and sunflower seeds, thyme, yeast extract

B2 (Riboflavin): kudzu, parsley, sesame seeds, spearmint, wheat bran, yeast extract

B3 (Niacin): bran (rice, wheat), kudzu, yeast extract

B5 (Pantothenic acid): bran (rice & wheat), sunflower seeds

B6 (Pyridoxine): bananas, basil, bran (rice, wheat), chives, dill, garlic, marjoram, molasses, oregano, rosemary, sage, savory, sesame seeds, sorghum, spearmint, sunflower seeds, tarragon

B9 (Folate): bananas, basil, broccoli, cantaloupe, chervil, collard greens, cowpeas, endive, flax seeds, marjoram, parsley, rosemary, spearmint, spinach, sunflower seeds, thyme, turnip greens, wheat germ, yeast extract

B12 (Cobalamin): found primarily in milk, meat, shellfish, and eggs, which are not suitable sources for herbivores. Fortunately, ruminants can synthesize B12 from cobalt, which is found in green leafy vegetables, comfrey leaves, and forage on soil that has sufficient cobalt levels.

Vitamin C: (can also by synthesized by livestock) broccoli, cantaloupe, citrus (fruit and rind), dried basil, kale, mustard greens, parsley, rose hips, rosemary, thyme, tomatoes

Vitamin D: sunshine

Vitamin E: basil, oregano, parsley, sage, sunflower seeds, thyme

Vitamin K: basil, beet greens, blackberries, blueberries, broccoli, cabbage, carrots, collard greens, dandelion greens, figs, kale, marjoram, mustard greens, oregano, parsley, raspberries, sage, Swiss chard, thyme, turnip greens

Minerals

Calcium: amaranth leaves, basil, celery seed, chamomile, chervil, chicory, cleavers, collard greens, coltsfoot, comfrey, coriander seeds, dandelion greens, dill, fennel seeds, flax seeds, horsetail, kale, kudzu, marjoram, mustard, mustard greens, oregano, parsley, plantain, poppy seed, rosemary, sage, savory, sesame seeds, sorrel, spearmint, thyme, turnip greens, willow

Cobalt: precursor to vitamin B12. Ruminants can synthesize B12 if they get enough cobalt in their diet. Found in green leafy vegetables and plants grown on cobalt-sufficient soil.

Copper: basil, burdock, chickweed, chicory, cleavers, coriander leaf, dandelion, dill, fennel seed, garlic, horseradish, marjoram, oregano, parsley, pumpkin seeds, savory, sesame seeds, sorrel, spearmint, sunflower seeds, thyme, winter squash seeds, yarrow

Iodine: primarily kelp and other seaweeds, which would be a stock-up item for most of us. Small amounts found in asparagus, cleavers, dandelion, garlic

Iron: anise seed, asparagus, bamboo, basil, blackberry, burdock, chervil, chicory, comfrey, coriander, cumin seed, dandelion, dill, fennel seeds, fenugreek seeds, kudzu, marjoram, nettle, oregano, parsley, pumpkin seeds, raspberry, rose, rosemary, savory, skullcap, sesame seeds, spearmint, strawberry, sunflower seeds, tarragon, thyme, turmeric, vervain, winter squash seeds, wormwood

Magnesium: basil, carrot leaves, coriander, dandelion, dill, elm, fennel seed, flax seeds, hop, marjoram, marshmallow, meadowsweet, molasses, mullein, oak, oat bran, oregano, parsley, pumpkin seeds, rice bran, rose, sage, savory, sesame seeds, slippery elm, spearmint, squash seeds, sunflower seeds, thyme, watermelon seeds, wheat bran

Manganese: bamboo, basil, coriander, dill, fennel, ginger, marjoram, oat bran, oregano, parsley, pumpkin seeds, rice bran, savory, sesame seeds, spearmint, squash seeds, sunflower seeds, thyme, wheat bran, wheat germ

Phosphorous: bran, chickweed, dill, flaxseed, goldenrod, marigold, pumpkin seeds, sesame seeds, squash seeds, sunflower seeds, wheat germ

Potassium: bananas, basil, borage, carrot leaves, chamomile, chervil, collards, coriander leaves, dandelion, dill, elder, fennel seeds, ginger, honeysuckle, kale, marjoram, meadowsweet, molasses, mullein, nettle, oak, oregano, couch grass, parsley, peppermint, plantain, pumpkin seeds, rice bran, skullcap, spearmint, spinach, squash seeds, sunflower seeds, Swiss chard, watermelon seeds, wormwood

Selenium: chervil, coriander, dill seeds, fenugreek, garlic, ginger, oat bran, parsley, rice bran, sunflower seeds, wheat bran

Sodium: usually obtained from mineral blocks or mixes, but also found in cleavers, clover, comfrey, dill, fennel, garlic, marshmallow, nettle, violet, woodruff

Zinc: basil, buckwheat, chervil, coriander, coriander seeds, fennel seeds, dill seeds, ginger, parsley, pumpkin seeds, sage, savory, sesame seeds, squash seeds, thyme, watermelon seeds, wheat germ

LAST BUT NOT LEAST—WATER

All animals should have unrestricted access to fresh, clean water at all times. This is especially true in hot, humid weather, but no less important at other times of the year. Actual consumption will depend on the time of year, their condition (growing, pregnant, or adult), and the kind of forage available. In general, your water buckets, stock tanks, or waterers should be able to accommodate the following approximate daily amounts per animal:

Cattle: 20 to 30 gallons

Goats and sheep: 2 gallons

Pigs: 3 to 6 gallons

Poultry: 1 gallon (per flock)

Rabbits: 1 cup

Animals won't always drink this much and sometimes they'll drink more. The best practice is to routinely check on water, making sure it's crystal clean. Dirty water can be used to water trees, shrubs, and other plants.

As you can see, there are quite a few options for feeding your livestock yourself. Working toward that goal will require some experimentation as you work on soil and pasture improvement, plus learn what grows best in your area. If you're new to livestock, I recommend starting with good-quality packaged feed and minerals, and then gradually adding homestead-grown foods to their diet.

CHAPTER 5

BREEDING AND PREGNANCY

Maintaining on ongoing supply of eggs, milk, and meat requires decision-making and planning. Chickens will lay eggs without a rooster, but milk and a yearly meat supply will require a male of your chosen species. This chapter will discuss the pros and cons of keeping males, how to know the best times for breeding, how to tell when your ladies are in season, how to detect pregnancy, and basic care during pregnancy.

KEEPING MALES

Males are necessary for reproduction, but tend to be larger and more aggressive than their female counterparts. Management techniques vary for the different species, so I'll start with poultry, then discuss rabbits, and finally, larger livestock.

Poultry

Poultry reproduction is based on broodiness, or the tendency to sit on and hatch eggs. Like the heat cycles of other species, broodiness is triggered by hormones, but there is no broody cycle. There is no way of knowing if or when a hen will go broody. Some breeds have a stronger tendency toward broodiness and mothering than others do, but individuals within each breed vary as well. For this reason, males are usually kept with the females as an integrated flock.

A good rooster, tom, gander, or drake will not only keep you supplied with fertile eggs for increase but will act as watch guardian. When our rooster makes a certain cluck, all our hens run for cover. Roosters will also search out tidbits for their ladies, and cluck for them to come when something tasty is found.

How do you choose a good flock sire from all those cute little chicks you're raising? We look for one that isn't too friendly as a youngster. Does that sound odd? Let me explain. While it's endearing to have a young rooster come up to eat out of your hand, in reality this in not friendliness, it's boldness. A bold rooster has little respect for humans and often exhibits aggressiveness as he gets older. An aggressive rooster will attack anything with his spurs that he deems a threat—including chicken keepers. From my experience, the best roosters are the ones who appear aloof when they are young. They respect my space and I respect theirs.

Rooster

In many urban areas, hens are allowed but not roosters. The case against them is their crowing. And it's true, they crow loudly at all hours. Urban chickens will still supply eggs, but when the time comes, you will need to replace them without the benefit of breeding your own.

What if you don't want or need more chicks? The easiest way to control your poultry population is by removing the broody's eggs, assuming you can find them! More than one farmer or homesteader has been surprised by a previously disappeared hen or duck who proudly shows up with a dozen or so babies following behind her.

While broodies don't bother anybody, they do stop laying while setting. If too many of your hens become broody at the same time, you will see a decrease in egg production. Some people will refer to "breaking broodiness," but this isn't as easy as it sounds. A broody hen is extremely persistent. Breaking broodiness usually involves exposing her bottom to low temperatures. This can be done with a mesh- or screen-bottomed cage, by filling her nest with frozen golf balls, or with a cold-water dunk. Sometimes this works, sometimes it doesn't.

Rabbits

Male and female rabbits are kept separate until breeding time. The doe is brought to the buck, because does tend to be very territorial and may attack a suitor if he intrudes on her space.

You will want to witness the breeding and remove the doe when they are done. If she's receptive, she will lift her tail and allow him to mount her. He'll fall off to the side when he's done. After a couple of times, she's ready to be put back in her own home. A repeat breeding in about 10 hours is recommended to further guarantee success.

Larger Livestock

What about larger livestock: bulls, bucks, rams, and boars? They are certainly the largest, heaviest, and strongest of their breeds. While it's possible to keep a buck, ram, or boar with the herd, it is usually desirable to keep track of who the sire is (if you have more than one), plus control the frequency and timing of birthing. Once the babies are born, there is also the question of how well adult males will accept them. When keeping males then, it is usually advantageous to keep the boys separate from the girls. This means they will need their own shelter, pastures with good fences, and pens. In addition, herd animals require like companionship for good mental health. A lone bull, buck, or ram will be miserable. That doesn't mean you need to keep two intact males. A neutered male will meet the need for companionship without having to keep more than one breeding animal.

If you don't have the space for separate pasture and housing, an alternative for bucks and rams is an anti-mating apron. These are tied around the torso and have a canvas or leather apron that hangs down. The herd sire lives with the does or ewes, but if he mounts one of them, the apron is in the way and prevents a successful mating. Simply remove the apron when you are ready to schedule a breeding. See Chapter 5 Resources on page 213 for where to find these.

Cows, does, ewes, and sows have hormonal heat cycles that determine when they are receptive to a male. Their male counterparts don't have such cycles; rather, their urge to mate is triggered by the scent of the females in heat. Rut is the male counterpart to that heat, and even a gentle male will become more aggressive and harder to handle. The standard rule is to never turn your back on them, especially during mating season. This is important, so I'll repeat it. Respect your boys' raw strength and unpredictability, and never turn your back on them.

Bucks in rut have the additional disadvantage of a disagreeably strong odor. This is partly because of scent glands located behind their horns, and partly because they have the rude habit of peeing on their own faces and beards to heighten their bucky cologne. In other words, when in rut, bucks stink. Rams and bulls don't have such a pronounced problem.

Other Considerations

If keeping a herd sire isn't feasible, however, there are still other options.

Stud Service

One alternative is to buy or trade for stud service. It will require travel, so distance is an important consideration here.

Services vary in their arrangements, so you will need to check for options when you contact the breeder. Some will lease the stud to you for a specified amount of time; some will require you to bring your girls to them. If your cow, doe, gilt, ewe, or sow needs an extended visit to allow for repeated breeding attempts, a daily boarding fee may apply. A length of stay commonly encompasses two heat cycles. The other option is to make another appointment and repeat the visit on another day.

A contract may be required. It will spell out exactly what you can expect and what is expected of you, including prices, other costs, and what happens if pregnancy doesn't result. You may be asked to show proof that your herd is free of specific diseases. You should expect the same from the stud's owner.

If you keep your own males, then you can be the one offering stud service.

Artificial Insemination

Another alternative may be to purchase semen to artificially inseminate your mothers-to-be. This option is also desirable to avoid inbreeding or otherwise expand your herd's gene pool. Theoretically this could be a do-it-yourself job, but because of its fair-to-middling success rate, it would be wise to enlist the help of a veterinarian experienced in the procedure.

WHEN TO BREED

When is the best time to breed? Spring is usually the season of chicks and lambs, but other times of the year may work better for you. Seasonal weather at the time of birthing may be a factor; for example, cold winters pose more risk for newborn hypothermia, while hot, wet weather increases the risk of coccidiosis. Seasonal activities, such as planting or harvesting, may be a factor in your best breeding time as well.

Livestock are considered either seasonal or aseasonal (non-seasonal) breeders. In seasonal breeders, daylight usually triggers estrus. This is the technical term for heat (also referred to as "in season"). Most goats and sheep are seasonal breeders with autumn being their primary time of fertility.

Some species are able and willing to breed any time of year, such as cows, pigs, rabbits, and some breeds of sheep and goats. These non-seasonal breeders will continue their estrus cycle throughout the year, although it may be more pronounced at some times than others. The reproductive cycles for livestock are:

Cattle: 21 days	*Pigs:* 21 days
Goats: 21 days	*Sheep:* 17 days

Rabbits do not have estrous cycles, rather, they are induced ovulators. The doe will usually ovulate when mated to a buck.

Poultry also have no estrus cycle, because broodiness is a hormonal response unrelated to breeding. Typically, however, poultry go broody during summer.

It is important that your breeding stock is healthy and in top shape before pregnancy. This is important to avoid complications and other health problems with both mothers and newborns. Pregnancy and lactation are physically demanding and not a time to play catch-up on health issues.

When to time breeding is determined by when you want young. Choose when you'd like birthing to take place and plan backward to determine the best time to breed. See the chart on page 100 for gestation lengths of various livestock.

HOW TO TELL WHEN YOUR LADIES ARE IN SEASON

How do you know when your gal is ready for a little romance? In general, she will show a distinct interest in the boys. At the peak of her cycle, she will stand still and allow a male to mount her. This is referred to as "standing heat." If she's not in heat, she will show no interest in a prospective suitor.

Other clues to look for in cows:

* Restless
* Very vocal and bellowing
* Change in personality
* Mounting other cows or allowing them to mount her
* Decrease in appetite
* Decreased milk production
* Swelling and reddening of vulva
* Vaginal discharge
* Sniffing and licking other cows

Other clues to look for in goats:

* Vigorous tail wagging (called flagging)
* Very vocal
* Decreased milk production
* Decreased interest in food
* Frequent urination
* Vaginal discharge
* Change in personality
* Mounting other does
* Interested in the scent of a buck rag (a rag that has been rubbed on the scent glands of a buck)

Other clues to look for in sheep:

* Generally less obvious than cattle or goats
* Tail wagging
* Increased interest in the rams

Other clues to look for in pigs:

- Restless
- Very vocal
- Mounts other sows
- Vaginal discharge
- Decreased interest in food

Other clues to look for in rabbits:

- Vaginal opening reddish-pink and moist
- Receptive to and cooperative with the buck

All of these signs can vary with the individual. Some will be more demonstrative than others, and a few will have what is known as "silent heats." These are the most difficult to breed, because they give very few clues that they are receptive. You may have to resort to trial and error, or keep her with a male through at least two heat cycles.

DETECTING PREGNANCY

Is she or isn't she? When you're hoping for a successful mating, that's always the question! The first clue will be that she stops going into heat, although that isn't necessarily a sure thing. The most accurate way to know is through a blood or urine test or ultrasound.

For a blood test, you can either draw the samples yourself and send them to the lab of your choice or have your veterinarian do it. The urine test is do-it-yourself. It detects the presence of estrone sulfate, a hormone produced by the placenta of pregnant females, including cows, goats, sheep, and pigs. A human pregnancy test will not work, because it measures human chorionic gonadotropin, a hormone that livestock don't produce.

For cattle, a rectal exam can determine the size and position of the uterus. These are most accurate after day 45 of the pregnancy.

In pigs, the sow's clitoris is visible because it is external; it will begin to point upward as her uterus sinks with the weight of unborn piglets. I did not find this to be the case with my sow, but it is said to generally be true.

For rabbits, a change in behavior is usually the best clue besides palpating baby bumps. The doe will become more moody and exhibit digging and nest-making behavior. If placed with a buck at this time she will growl at him and be unwilling to cooperate.

For goats and sheep, an enlarged abdomen may or may not indicate pregnancy. A well-fed belly can also bulge with food, and normal rumen activity can look like fetal movement.

Once you have a probable conception date circled on your calendar, how long will it be until you can expect your farm babies? Use the following chart to help you calculate the due dates of your livestock.

GESTATION TIME FOR LIVESTOCK

ANIMAL	GESTATION TIME (APPROXIMATE)
COWS	280 to 290 days, depending on breed size
GOATS	145 to 155 days; smaller breeds tend to have shorter pregnancies
PIGS	114 days, best remembered as 3 months, 3 weeks, 3 days
RABBITS	31 to 32 days
SHEEP	145 to 147 days

There are numerous online calculators that will help you figure a due date. Web links are in Resources.

CARE DURING PREGNANCY

Healthy mothers-to-be don't require special care, but they do need adequate nutrition from good quality feed and forage and plenty of exercise. Overfeeding during the first two trimesters of pregnancy can cause delivery problems due to maternal obesity and a large baby. Toward the end of a pregnancy, expectant mothers need adequate protein and calcium, but also carbohydrates. Begin to increase feed gradually during this time. Grain is often recommended, but if you increase grain, increase calcium-rich foods too. See Diet-Related Problems on page 110.

Keep good-quality minerals available at all times. If your soil is deficient in any of these, you may need to add individual minerals to your free-choice offerings. Selenium is especially noteworthy, because a deficiency can cause abortions, stillbirths, retained placenta, and a paralysis in newborns called white muscle disease. In selenium-deficient areas, selenium is often administered by injection (a prescription item) or as an oral gel prior to birthing.

If you are using chemical dewormers, make sure they are safe to use during pregnancy.

If you vaccinate, give these two weeks prior to the due date. This will give the newborns protection as well.

Ruminants should be dried off from milking two months before birthing. This allows the mother to put all her energies into the final growth of her babies. Since supply is based on demand, start by taking less milk at each milking. Gradually decrease the frequency of milking going to once a day or every other day, then every two days, etc.

Sows tend toward constipation at the end of their pregnancy, so high-fiber foods such as bran, alfalfa, and/or beet pellets are recommended.

Rabbits have a short pregnancy, just 31 to 33 days. She needs good nutrition and a nest box. Shortly before she kindles, she will create a nest of straw and fur.

What do you need to do next? Read on!

CHAPTER 6

BLESSED EVENTS: BIRTHING AND HATCHING

The big day is approaching! How do you need to prepare? What can you expect? This chapter will help you get ready for birthing and hatching, know what to expect, plus help you identify some common problems. My information will be a general introduction, however, so I highly recommend that you invest in books specific to your livestock of choice.

BEFORE BIRTH: IMPORTANT SUPPLIES

If you've researched supply lists for livestock, you've probably noticed that they vary, and often depend on the list maker's experience. In general, here are some things that are good to have on hand for the birth.

BIRTHING SUPPLIES

ANIMAL	GENERAL SUPPLIES	JUST IN CASE
COWS	Good barn lighting or battery lantern, flashlights, headlights	Veterinarian's emergency phone numbers
	Extra batteries	Cell phone
	Betadine or 7% iodine for treating umbilical cords	Bucket large enough to mix disinfectant in water
	Baby food jar for holding umbilical cord dip	Source for warm water
		Iodine-based disinfectant or scrub
	Bulb syringe for clearing out nose and mouth	OB gloves if assistance is needed
	Old towels and clean rags for rubbing down newborns and wiping your hands	OB lubricant
		Puller to assist with malpresentation
	Halter to fit your cow and tie rope	Tubing bag or esophageal feeder
	Camera (optional)	Frozen colostrum or colostrum replacer
		Calf nipples and bottle
GOATS AND SHEEP	Good barn lighting or battery lantern, flashlights, headlamps	Veterinarian's emergency phone numbers
	Extra batteries	Cell phone
	Old towels and wash cloths, rather than disposable pads, for rubbing down newborns and wiping your hands	OB gloves if assistance is needed
		OB lubricant
	Blunt-nose scissors for cutting umbilical cords	Puller to assist with malpresentation
	Nasal aspirator to clear airways if needed	Feeding tube and syringe
	Betadine for treating umbilical cords	Frozen colostrum or colostrum replacer
	Selenium/vitamin E gel if you are in a selenium-deficient area	Nutri-Drench or Goats Prefer Calcium Drench for weak babies or mom
	Scale for weighing kids (optional)	Pritchard nipples and bottles to fit
	Notebook and pen for recording birth times and weights	
	Kid or lamb sweaters if the weather is cold	
	Camera (optional)	
	Molasses, blackstrap or old-fashioned. Mix a glug in warm water to offer the doe or ewe after birthing.	

BIRTHING SUPPLIES

ANIMAL	GENERAL SUPPLIES	JUST IN CASE
PIGS	Good barn lighting or battery lantern, flashlights, headlamps	Veterinarian's emergency phone numbers
	Extra batteries	Cell phone
		OB gloves if assistance is needed
		OB lubricant
		Frozen colostrum or colostrum replacer (may use from a cow or goat if necessary)
RABBITS	Nest box with straw or hay in the bottom	Mineral oil, for stuck kits

If you have an emergency, you can hopefully get a vet out in time, but check with your vet beforehand to see what emergency supplies and medications they recommend you keep on hand. They can instruct on what to do while they are on the way.

These are suggested emergency supplies for cows, goats, and sheep:

- Calcium gluconate injectable, given subcutaneously for milk fever, also known as hypocalcemia (see Common Problems on page 109). Sometimes given IV.

- Injectable antibiotic, given after an assisted birth. Veterinary-grade antibiotics are available without prescription from a feed store or via mail order from livestock supply companies. LA-200 is a broad-spectrum antibiotic that doesn't require refrigeration.

- Sterile syringes in a variety of sizes, from 3 to 60 cc

- Sterile needles in a variety of sizes, from 16 to 18 gauge; 1 to 1.5 inches in length

- CMPK drench or gel (calcium, magnesium, phosphorus, potassium) for milk fever

- Propylene glycol to treat ketosis

- Sterile syringes in a variety of sizes, from 3 to 60 cc

- Sterile needles in a variety of sizes, from 16 to 18 gauge; 1 to 1.5 inches in length.

These are suggested emergency supplies for pigs:

- Sterile syringes in a variety of sizes, from 3 to 60 cc

- Sterile needles in a variety of sizes, from 16 to 18 gauge; 1 to 1.5 inches in length. For piglets, use 18-gauge, ½-inch needles.

- Oxytocin is the most common drug used in difficult farrowing, but it requires a prescription.

Disposable Diapers and Pads

Disposable diapers and pads are very popular for birthing events. They are used to catch the baby and the placenta, and then tossed into a plastic trash bag so that there is no mess to clean up. From a prepper's point of view, there are two things to consider. The first is having to stock up on these disposable items. The second is getting rid of them. If you have a trash or garbage service available, or are able to make it to the landfill, no problem. But if SHTF, these conveniences may be gone. If you go the stock-up route, be sure to have a plan to dispose of that trash bag. The blood-soaked rags, afterbirth, and membranes will begin to smell as they decompose and attract flies and carnivores.

PREPARE THE BIRTHING AREA

For ruminants, a separate birthing stall is a good idea. It should be large enough for the laboring mother, several newborns, and you. It provides a clean, safe, private area for birthing and bonding, plus protects new babies from being pushed around or stepped on by the others. Location should be convenient for you but not isolated from the rest of the herd. Herd animals become stressed if they can't see and smell one another.

About a week before your girl's due date, put her in the birthing stall at night. This makes it easier to check on her, and if she's early, she has a protected area for her labor and delivery. Clean the stall daily and make sure her water bucket is high enough to prevent newborns from accidentally falling in.

For pigs, farrowing crates are sometimes used to allow the sow to lie down to feed her piglets, but not walk around and possibly step on them. Most natural pig keepers, however, do not use them, but allow plenty of room for the birth.

For rabbits, the doe is given the nest box on her twenty-eighth day of gestation. With only a few days to go, her nesting instincts are strong and she's ready to prepare it for kindling.

STAGES OF BIRTH

Labor

Early labor is similar for most farm animals. As their due date approaches, any of the following changes may be a clue that delivery is getting close:

* Udder begins to fill out (This is known as "bagging up." It sometimes happens days or weeks before labor.)

* Restlessness

* Isolates from the others

* Decreased interest in food

* Appears preoccupied

* Nesting behavior

* Ruminants may paw the ground

* Pigs will gather and pile up straw or hay

* Rabbits will pull their fur to line the nest box

* Discharge: mucous at first, tinged with blood when birthing is close

* Swollen vulva

Birth

Pushing indicates the birth is in progress in ruminants. Her tail will rise with each contraction. She may deliver standing up or lying down. You may see the water sac first unless it breaks in utero. For cows, the most common presentation is front feet first, although hind feet first is also considered normal. Goats and ewes typically deliver either front or back feet first; both are considered normal. Twins are often born front feet for one, back feet for the other. If all goes well, all you need to do is watch.

For pigs, the sow will lie on her side and remain still during the birth of her piglets. They will instinctively move toward her warm belly and milk.

Rabbits prefer privacy and nothing may happen if you are there watching. Check the nest box for kits on day 31, and remove any stillborns and uneaten placentas.

LABOR AND OFFSPRING FOR LIVESTOCK

	LENGTH OF LABOR, FROM HARD CONTRACTIONS TO BIRTH	NUMBER OF NEWBORNS TO EXPECT
COWS	30 minutes to 2 hours	One calf; sometimes twins
GOATS	30 minutes	Singles, twins, or triplets; quads or quints may occur with Nigerian Dwarfs or Kinders
PIGS	Less than 2 hours, 30 minutes	6 to 12 piglets
RABBITS	10 to 60 minutes	Standard-size meat rabbits typically have 6 to 12 bunnies
SHEEP	1 to 2 hours	Singles or twins

Most of the time all goes well. You can help dry babies off, and make sure they can find a teat and get a tummy full of colostrum. Clean up any soiled straw, add fresh bedding, and offer feed to the new mother. Goats are commonly given a gallon bucket of warm water mixed with a glug of molasses.

After Birth: Caring for a Newborn

Follow these steps after birth.

* Wipe birth membranes from nose and mouth.

* Clear airways with the bulb syringe aspirator if needed.

* Care for the umbilical cord: dip the end of the cord in betadine dip.

* Towel off to dry.

* Examine for deformities.

* Make sure they can find a teat on their own.

* Prevent hypothermia if it's cold: use a heat lamp, kid or lamb coats, or old child-size sweatshirts. Make sure pigs have plenty of straw bedding.

* Observe for maternal bonding or rejection. A reluctant first-time mother may need a little coaxing or to be held while her newborns nurse for the first time.

Newborn piglets are often given iron injections. Ask your veterinarian if you should do this.

Expulsion of Placenta

This is the last stage of labor. For twins or triplets, it's not uncommon for each to have a separate placenta. Some animals, such as goats and pigs, may eat it. A retained placenta can cause infection. If it is not expelled within the following times, consult your vet.

Cows: within 12 to 24 hours

Goats: within 12 to 24 hours

Sheep: within 12 to 18 hours

Pigs: within 2 to 4 hours

Rabbits: within 60 minutes

COMMON PROBLEMS

If hard contractions do not produce babies within the expected time range, you (or someone) will need to assist. You will need to use the scrub, gloves, and lubricant in your birthing kit, gently insert your hand into the birth canal, and try to figure out what is going on. Descriptions of common problems are listed below. Livestock keepers frequently handle these themselves, but if you are uncertain about your findings or otherwise feel you could use help, do not hesitate to call your vet.

Malpresentation

This is when the fetus is in the wrong position to deliver normally. It may be that one or both legs are back, the head is turned, or it is a tail presentation (true breech). If labor takes longer than the times listed above, then this may be the problem. Assistance will be required or both babies and mother will die. Wash up with hot soapy water and disinfectant, put on gloves and OB lubricant, and gently slip your hand into the birth canal. Take a deep breath, relax, and gently try to feel for feet, noses, or tails. For cows, does, and ewes, you need to find two feet and pull the baby out. For pigs or rabbits, a piglet or kit may be stuck in the birth canal and will need to be pulled out. If you have to pull, pull with the contractions.

Simultaneous Birth

If you see four feet sticking out of the birth canal, it is twins trying to be born at the same time. You will need to push one twin back and pull out the other first.

Stillbirths

Sometimes babies are born dead. The cause may be prolonged or difficult labor, a congenital problem, problems with the placenta or umbilical cord, disease, or nutritional imbalance. Sometimes this happens even if you've tried to do your best. Sometimes it's just a fact of life. If you have concerns, check with your veterinarian. Usually it is a one-time event and following pregnancies are successful. If the stillborn was a single, the mother will look for it and grieve.

If you have a rejected or orphaned baby, or a twin or triplet, it may be possible to graft it onto the stillborn's mother. Tricks include rubbing the live baby with afterbirth or the mother's urine. Cattle people will sometimes skin the dead calf and use the skin as a coat on the calf being grafted. Feed the foster mother to distract her while the new baby nurses. If she's reluctant, tie her head and do this four times a day. Once her milk passes through her adoptee, it will smell as if it belongs to her. She should accept it as her own after that.

Rejection

Sometimes a dam simply will not accept her newborn. If she is a first-time mother, she may need to be coaxed to let her baby nurse. Once she gets used to it, there is usually no further problem. If she continues to reject it, your choices are to either raise it as a bottle baby, or try to graft it onto an adoptive mother (see page 116).

Diet-Related Problems

Two life-threatening problems that can occur shortly before or after delivery are related to diet: ketosis (pregnancy toxemia or twin lamb disease), and hypocalcemia (milk fever). They can cause stillbirths as well as death to the mother if not recognized immediately and treated. Fortunately, both are preventable. The following information will help you with identification, treatment, and prevention of both.

Ketosis

Ketosis is a metabolic condition that results when the body's demand for energy (carbohydrates) exceeds what the diet provides. It usually happens late in pregnancy when the babies are rapidly growing. If the dam isn't consuming enough carbohydrates to meet the need, her body begins to metabolize fat for energy. Ketones are the byproduct of fat metabolism. As ketones accumulate, the system becomes increasingly acidic to the point where it can be fatal. Ketosis is more common in overweight and confined animals than in animals that get plenty of pasture and exercise.

A mother with ketosis may stop eating; become sluggish, not alert, and disinterested in her surroundings; and may prefer to lie down. Treat with either propylene glycol or 1 part molasses to 2 parts corn syrup. For goats, you can use Nutri-Drench or Goats Prefer Calcium Drench. Additionally, give the following:

* B vitamin injections to stimulate appetite
* Probiotics, yogurt, or kefir to reestablish digestive flora in the rumen
* Water—drench if necessary; she needs water to flush the ketones out of her system
* Continue treatment until she is eating on her own with good appetite

To prevent ketosis during pregnancy, provide plenty of pasture forage and high-quality hay. Make sure the animals get plenty of exercise.

Hypocalcemia or Milk Fever

This condition has nothing to do with fever, but rather with an improper calcium-to-phosphorous ratio in the diet. Grain is usually the culprit here, because it is high in phosphorous but low in calcium. The condition occurs toward the end of pregnancy, when the babies need calcium for bone development, or immediately after birthing when milk production kicks in. If the mother can't get enough calcium through her diet, her body will begin to deplete its own resources. Besides bones and teeth, calcium is necessary for proper muscle function (skeletal, heart, digestive, uterine). With a calcium shortage, muscles become weak so that the dam can no longer stand, digestion slows, uterine contractions weaken, and eventually, her heart will give out if the problem isn't corrected immediately. Typically, the mother with hypocalcemia will go off her grain first, then stop eating hay. The other symptoms of hypocalcemia are very similar to ketosis, so it is recommended to treat hypocalcemia as you would treat ketosis. In addition, give calcium gluconate injections or IV. See product label for dosages.

To prevent hypocalcemia, total dietary intake should contain 2 to 2.5 parts calcium to 1 part phosphorous. Calcium can be provided in alfalfa, clover, comfrey, or kudzu hay, or by top dressing her feed with dolomite powder or ground limestone. Don't increase grain dramatically, increase forage and high-quality hay instead. If you do increase grain, also increase calcium.

INTRODUCING NEWBORNS TO THE OTHERS

A separate birthing area is a temporary arrangement, usually used for about 24 hours or so to allow for bonding. Once you're satisfied that the newborns are sturdy on their feet and nursing well, you will want to introduce them to the others. If the birthing stall is nearby, the rest of the herd or flock will already know the newborns by sight and smell. Even so, they will be curious and you can expect some scuffling and hollering as a new social order gets worked out.

Most mothers will be quick to defend their young, although some don't. That's why you need to supervise introductions. Socializing includes learning that it isn't acceptable to get milk from any teat and whose way to stay out of. Some butting is common, but most adults are relatively gentle in their admonitions of the babies. Keep an eye out for bullying. Occasionally one will be too rough and cause injury. These need to be separated until the young are quick enough on their feet to stay out of the way.

With our pigs, we initially kept our boar separate from Polly and her piglets, because we didn't know if he would accept them. One day the piglets wiggled out under the gate and we found them attempting to nurse from dad. He just laid there, so it was a relief to see he didn't mind them. We reunited our breeding pair briefly, until we realized that Waldo wouldn't share the feed. We kept them separate after that.

DAIRY ANIMALS: MANAGING TRIPLETS AND QUADS

Cows and sheep typically give birth to singles or twins. Goats typically have twins, but triplets are common and, occasionally, quadruplets. Multiples are more common with Nigerian Dwarfs, Pygmies, and Kinders, and the concern is that each kid gets enough milk. Monitor their weight gain and behavior to ensure they are getting enough. A hungry kid won't gain weight and will cry for milk. In addition, here are a couple of ideas for managing multiples.

Bottle feeding

Bottle feeding. Bucklings are usually more aggressive feeders than their sisters are, so they make good candidates for bottle feeding. Choose one (if triplets) or two (if quads) and train them to the bottle at birth. You may need the milk from another doe if their mother is not producing enough on her own.

Another advantage to this is that bucklings need to be separated from their dams earlier than doelings, because they are capable of mating as young as eight weeks. A bottle-fed buckling will miss his mother, but with less hollering than with a cold-turkey weaning.

Nighttime rotation of kids. Once the kids are about two weeks of age and nibbling hay, you can separate the biggest and strongest at night in a pen near their mother and siblings. This allows the smaller kids of the litter to get all the milk during the night. If all kids are growing well, you can rotate which are separated.

HATCHING EGGS

Home hatching of poultry is one of the best ways to expand your flock or replace elderly birds. You can either use an incubator or let a broody hen do the job.

It's far easier to let the broody do the work, because she will instinctively monitor the temperature of the eggs and turn them. When the chicks hatch, she'll keep them warm, find food for them, keep their bottoms clean, and protect them fiercely. However, the results are less predictable.

A Note About Hen-Hatched Eggs

In general, a hen will lay over a period of several days, one egg per day. After the first chick hatches, she will remain on the nest for the others to hatch. After several days, she will leave the nest to tend to her chicks. Any remaining eggs should be discarded.

An incubator will generally give better results. It will require monitoring the temperature and humidity, plus periodic turning of the eggs (follow the manufacturer's instructions for set-up and care of the eggs). It will require energy to power, as will a heat lamp to keep the babies warm after they hatch. If you choose to incubate your eggs, you can calculate a hatching date using the following incubation times:

African geese: 31 days

Geese (general): 29 to 30 days

Bantams: 19 to 21 days

Guinea fowl: 24 to 25 days

Chickens: 21 days

Mallards: 26.5 days

Chinese geese: 31 days

Muscovies: 35 days

Ducks (general): 28 to 30 days

Turkey: 28 days

It will be your job to feed and care for the babies, although it is possible to graft chicks onto a broody hen (see page 116).

To care for mail-order or incubator-hatched chicks, poults, keets, ducklings, goslings, etc., you'll need the following supplies:

❋ Bedding: For the first few days cover the bottom with paper towels (newspaper is too slippery). After several days, you can use pine shavings, chopped straw, or sand.

❋ Brooder box: This can be a large cardboard box, large plastic tote, metal washtub, or large metal trough to serve as a brooding area. The sides should be at least 12 inches high to protect the hatchlings from drafts and to prevent them from jumping out.

❋ Heat lamp to attach or hang above the brooder box. A regular 60- to 100-watt light bulb can be used.

❋ Screen or hardware cloth to cover the top of the box

❋ Thermometer to monitor temperature in the box. Initially it should be 90 to 95°F (32 to 35°C) for the first week. Adjust the temperature in the brooder box by raising or lowering the light. Decrease temperature by 5 degrees each week until about 70°F (21°C). By the time the babies are fully feathered, they should be able to maintain their own body temperature.

For both hen- and hand-raised babies, you'll need:

❋ Chick feeder

❋ Chick waterer

❋ Electrolytes, powdered, added to water of mail-order chicks their first several days

❋ Feed (see page 116)

❋ Grit, chick-sized gravel for chicks to eat for digestion of grain

GRAFTING ONTO A BROODY HEN

Whether you have mail ordered baby birds or hatched them in an incubator, an excellent way to raise chicks, ducklings, poults, goslings, and keets is by grafting onto a broody chicken. The key to successful grafting is to do it at night, when all is dark and quiet. Gently slip the babies under her. They will instinctively nestle under her for warmth. There is no guarantee with this method, but it usually works.

This works with any poultry hatchlings, and an adoptive hen will meet their needs for warmth, food, water and protection as though they are chickens. Eventually their natural instincts will take over. I'll never forget how surprised our Mama Buff Orpington was when her adopted ducklings first saw the chickens' large water dish. They made a mad dash and dived right in! But they still followed Mama Hen around and settled under her at night. She accepted the strange behavior of her brood, and everybody was happy.

FEEDING HATCHLINGS

Mammals provide milk for their young, but birds do not. Wild birds nurture their young in a nest until they are old enough to fly, but domesticated poultry have the instincts to scratch and peck for food within their first couple of days of life. This is what makes mail ordering and hand raising chicks, ducklings, poults, and keets possible. As with other livestock feeds, commercial chick feed is available for purchase. Or you can make your own.

Chicks are small, so they need small pieces. Whole grains and peas need to be cracked into fine pieces. This is possible with a hand grain mill set to a coarse grind. For example:

* barley
* corn
* dried peas
* lentils
* milo
* oats

- peanuts
- sunflower seeds
- triticale
- ground wheat berries

Small grains and seeds do not need grinding:

- amaranth
- millet
- flax seeds
- sesame seeds
- bran
- kelp meal

You can also feed them chopped cooked egg (a good source of protein), chopped fresh greens, and cooked cereals, such as oatmeal. Growing babies need more protein than adult birds. Here are daily protein requirements for young poultry (listed as percent of daily intake):

Chicks: 20%

Ducklings: 18 to 20%

Goslings: 20%

Keets: 24 to 26%

Poults: 24 to 28%

Protein requirements decrease as they get older. This is especially important for water fowl, which can develop wing problems with a high-protein diet.

Also, offer free-choice grit.

Pasty Bottom

If you hand raise your birds, you will need to keep an eye on their bottoms. Their soft droppings can harden on the soft down of their bottoms. If not removed it will block the anus, make it difficult to excrete waste, and kill them. Their mother will usually tend to this, but without one it will be their keeper's job to remove the crust that forms on their bottoms. Known as "pasty bottom" or "pasty butt," this is more of a problem when you are using commercial feeds.

INTRODUCING NEWCOMERS TO THE FLOCK

Introducing young birds to the existing flock is always a concern. It's also unpredictable. I have found that success largely depends on the personality of the rooster. In general, integrating newcomers is easiest when the youngsters have been raised in the coop. If they were hen-hatched, Mama Hen will not let the others bother her chicks. If they were mail ordered, place their brooder box and heat lamp inside the coop. This way the established flock can see and smell them, and will more readily accept that these youngsters belong there. There is still quite a bit of squabbling as the pecking order is reestablished, but they are not chased out of the coop.

CHAPTER 7

EGGS, MILK, AND MEAT

If you ask folks why they keep livestock, I'm guessing that near the top of almost every list is for food. More and more people want to eat healthy, naturally raised, minimally processed eggs, milk, and meat from humanely treated animals fed healthy, natural diets. Having a self-sustaining food supply is also important to many folks, including most preppers.

As with fruits and vegetables, the production of eggs, milk, and meat is seasonal. There is an ebb and flow to our homegrown food supply, but we must eat every day. Vegetables, fruits, eggs, milk, dairy products, and meat are perishable, so we must learn how to either extend their production or preserve them. This chapter will cover the basics of producing animal foods, how to aim for year-round production, and ways to preserve them.

EGGS

Hen laying eggs

Eggs are a seasonal food. Chickens and ducks are the most productive of the barnyard birds; guinea fowl, geese, meat-breed ducks, and turkeys less so—they lay during their hatching season only. Egg production is highest during long daylight hours, lowest when the days are short. Poultry don't lay when they are molting.

Eggs right out of the chicken have a natural protective coating known as the cuticle or bloom. The bloom coats the porous egg shell, protecting it from a potential invasion of bacteria. It is those bacteria that contaminate the egg contents, causing it to rot. Washing the egg removes the bloom and decreases the egg's shelf life.

Over time, the water content in the egg will evaporate through the pores in the shell, forming an air bubble within the egg. You can tell how fresh an egg is by placing it in a bowl of water. Fresh eggs will be heavy and lie on their sides on the bottom of the bowl. As the eggs age, one end will begin to turn upward. An egg that remains on the bottom but in an upright position is about at the end of its shelf life. Eggs that float need to be discarded.

How long will eggs keep without refrigeration or other preservation? That depends on room temperature. Eggs stored in a cool root cellar will keep longer than those stored on the countertop of a warm kitchen. Store your home fresh eggs in the coolest place you can. If in doubt, use the float test to determine freshness.

In managing your egg supply, you have several options: only use eggs in season, optimize conditions for year-round production of fresh eggs, or preserve eggs for times when poultry aren't laying.

How to Have a Year-Round Egg Supply

Artificial lighting. This is standard practice for commercial breeders, but more controversial amongst homestead or backyard poultry keepers. Chickens need light to produce eggs, and the natural cycle of the seasons allows for a rest from laying. If you live where daylight hours are exceptionally short during winter, that may seem too long to go without eggs.

An artificial light can make up for a daylight deficit. It doesn't have to be a glaring light, just enough for a human to read by. A 40-watt light bulb is enough for 100 square feet of chicken coop. The key is to ensure at least 16 hours of light per day (total daylight and artificial light) and 8 hours of darkness for nighttime roosting.

Winter-laying chickens. Australorp, Buckeye, Delaware, Dominique, Faverolles, Jersey Giant, New Hampshire, Orpington, Plymouth Rock, Rhode Island Red, Sussex, and Wyandotte are all considered winter layers. They won't be as prolific as during the summer, but they can still offer a winter egg supply.

Laying ducks. Egg-laying breeds of ducks such as Runners and Campbells are generally less sensitive to daylight fluctuations than chickens, and will often produce more than chickens. Ducks are more sensitive to temperature, however, and will lay less when the weather gets really cold.

PRESERVATION TECHNIQUES FOR EGGS

All eggs for preservation must be fresh and clean. Some techniques require that the bloom not be washed from the egg prior to preservation.

Freezing

Freezing eggs is an easy and simple way to preserve them. Of course, it requires electricity, but I include it here because of its simplicity and for those who may have a solar-powered or DC-battery powered freezer.

Beat eggs well, add salt if desired (½ teaspoon per cup of eggs), pour into ice cube trays or muffin tins, and freeze. One cube equals one small egg. One standard-size muffin tin cup will hold approximately two eggs. Thaw and use for baking, quiche, or scrambled eggs. If you wish, whites and yolks can be frozen separately.

Pickling

This is a preservation technique for hard-boiled eggs. Fill a wide-mouth jar with peeled hard-boiled eggs, cover with vinegar or leftover pickle juice, and allow to marinate at least one week in the fridge or root cellar. Unrefrigerated, these are said to keep for two weeks; refrigerated or in a chilly root cellar, they will keep for months. Very tasty in fresh salads, as deviled eggs, or in egg salad sandwiches.

Homemade pickled eggs

Dehydrating

This technique is more time consuming, but dried powdered eggs are very handy. You can use a dehydrator or a slow oven. Scrambled or raw eggs can be dehydrated, with special precautions for using powdered raw egg. Because of the fat content in egg yolk, dehydrated eggs don't keep as long as other dried foods.

To dehydrate scrambled eggs: Cook in a nonstick skillet, or use a saturated fat such as coconut oil, palm oil shortening, beef tallow, lard, or clarified butter. These are more stable and less prone to rancidity than vegetable oils. Spread the scrambled eggs on food dehydrator trays or baking sheets and dry at 145°F (63°C) until crisp and brittle. These are best if powdered in a blender once cool, because rehydrated chunks result in a rubbery scrambled egg.

To dehydrate raw eggs: Beat as for scrambled and pour onto fruit leather trays or baking sheets. Set dehydrator or oven to 145°F (63°C). Drying time is longer than for scrambled eggs. Powder in a blender. These can be added directly to batters or doughs with equal parts liquid. Powdered eggs must be cooked to a minimum of 160°F (71°C) to prevent possible problems with salmonella.

To store: Store in clean glass jars or containers. Without refrigeration, they will keep three to four months. Shelf life will be improved if they are kept in the refrigerator or freezer, or by vacuum packing.

To rehydrate: Mix equal parts powdered egg and warm water. Allow to sit at least 10 minutes before using.

To use: Dehydrated eggs must be thoroughly cooked before consuming. Once rehydrated these can be used in baking, scrambled, and for omelets or quiche.

Water Glassing

Before refrigeration, water glass was sold at hardware and drug stores for preserving fresh eggs. Also known as sodium silicate, water glass is a slippery, slightly alkaline liquid that is still used as a cement floor sealer and cardboard carton adhesive. It works because it prevents the water content of the egg from evaporating through the porous shell. If you can find water glass, then you can use it too. Use only fresh eggs free of cracks, dirt, and manure. Do not wash. Washing will remove the bloom and decrease the effectiveness of water glassing.

1) In the crock or jar, mix 11 parts water to 1 part water glass.

2) Add the eggs, submerging at least 2 inches below the liquid surface.

3) Date and cover the crock, and store in a cool place.

4) Water glass evaporates, so periodically check the crock and top off as needed.

To use: The eggs will be slippery when you remove them. Wash and break individually into a measuring cup or bowl to check for freshness. The whites will become thin the longer they are preserved, but the eggs are still good to use.

Shelf life can be up to five months under cool conditions, shorter if your air temperature is warmer.

Liming

This is another old-fashioned egg-storage method, and for me, preferable because pickling lime is more readily available than water glass. Pickling lime can be found in the canning supply section of any store that sells canning supplies. The proportions are:

* 16 parts water

* 1 part canning salt (or any non-iodized salt)

* 2 parts pickling lime (food-grade hydrated lime)

Mix until milky looking, and then add fresh, clean, unwashed, never-refrigerated eggs. Because of the salt, the eggs will float initially, and then sink. Date and cover the crock. Store in a cool place. Check the liquid level frequently, and top off as needed to keep the eggs submerged.

To use: The eggs will have a light coating of lime on the shells; wash this off. Break eggs individually into a measuring cup or bowl to check for freshness. The whites will become thinner the longer they are preserved, but the eggs are still good to use.

Shelf-life can be up to five months under cool conditions, shorter if your air temperature is warmer. In the South, I found that after about four months, the eggs developed a slightly metallic taste.

Larding or Oiling

Back in the day when folks kept hogs, larding eggs was a popular way to preserve them. Eggs were packed in a crock filled with lard, or coated with lard and packed in salt, sawdust, or oatmeal. The modern version is to use food-grade mineral oil, coconut oil, or butter. The eggs are stored in cartons or packed in salt, sawdust, or oatmeal.

To use: Wipe each egg and break into a measuring cup or bowl to check for freshness.

Other Uses for Surplus Eggs

You can sell or trade, but you can also feed surplus eggs to other animals.

Dogs and cats: beat as for scrambled and feed raw or cooked.

Poultry and pigs: hard-boil and chop with the shell intact.

Never feed whole eggs in the shell to any critter, unless you don't mind them helping themselves any time they find an egg on their own.

Other Possibilities

You can also preserve finished products that contain eggs. For example:

* Noodles: Homemade noodles are a good way to use up extra eggs, and they don't need refrigeration to store long term.

* Baked goods: Instead of preserving the eggs, preserve the things in which they are used, such as cakes, muffins, cookies, pancakes, and breakfast breads. Pop these in the freezer.

See also Off-Grid Storage of Eggs, Milk, and Meat (page 153) for more ideas.

MILK AND MILK PRODUCTS

Like eggs, fresh milk is seasonal. Individual dairy animals will produce well after giving birth and then taper off in accordance with their offspring's natural demands. With no human management, a natural weaning will take place as the young rely more on solid foods and less on milk. Eventually, milk production will stop unless we humans encourage it along. We do this by keeping up the demand through milking.

For the first several days after giving birth, dairy animals produce colostrum. It is rich in nutrients and antibodies, which are vital to good infant health. Gradually, milk replaces the colostrum, so plan to wait on milking for about a week. If she is producing more than her babies can consume, milk out colostrum to store in the freezer for future emergencies.

The first milk from a full udder will be thin with the highest water content. The cream is last, milked out when the udder is closer to empty.

Typically, dairy animals are bred once a year. They are allowed to produce milk for ten months and are dried off two months before the next calf or kid is due. This gives her body a rest and allows her extra calories to go to her fetus.

A cow will naturally produce milk for 10 to 11 months before drying off. She must be re-bred two months after she gives birth, because she has a 10-month pregnancy. With this practice, you will have fresh milk for about 10 months with a two-month dry spell.

A goat doe will typically produce milk for nine to ten months, although it is not uncommon for some does to have longer lactations. A goat has a five-month pregnancy, and it's customary to wait six months after she kids before re-breeding. As with a cow, the best practice is to dry her off for the last two months of her pregnancy.

A ewe (dairy sheep breed) will produce milk for about eight months. Standard practice is to milk for six months. At that time, she can be dried up and rebred. Because sheep produce less milk than goats, twice-a-day milking will keep up the milk demand and result in the best yield.

The Relationship of Feed to Milk Production

When an animal is in milk, she needs extra calories. Some people feed extra grain for maximum milk production, but as we've seen in Chapter 4, Forage and Feed, ruminants don't digest grain well. Understanding this has caused me to ask myself, do I need to push milk production to the limit, or can I learn to make do with what is being produced? If I need more, wouldn't it be better to keep a second or third doe in milk?

Pushing an animal to her production limits may make sense to commercial producers who replace stock frequently, but as a homesteader, I'd rather have less milk each year for a longer number of productive years. Even so, I have learned that the quality of forage and hay makes a noticeable difference in milk production. If my does get plenty of top-quality forage and hay, then I get plenty of milk.

THE MILKING PROCESS
Supplies

At the very least, you'll need a bucket and something to sit on! But here's a slightly more complete list. Many folks use disposable items for milking and milk filtering, such as paper towels, baby wipes, and disposable milk filters. These are options, but since we're talking prepper livestock in this book, my list contains reusable alternatives.

* A way to secure her head, such as a halter and tie, head gate, or milking stand

* Clean cotton cloths or handkerchiefs for udder washing and milk filters

* Container of warm water for udder washing (see Cleanliness on page 129)

* Feed bucket with feed to keep her occupied

* Glass jars for storing milk, gallon size for cows, ½-gallon size for goats

* Hobble (optional)

* Seamless, stainless steel bucket

* Stainless steel milk strainer

Milking Stands

For goats, sheep, and the smaller cow breeds you'll want a milking stand. Also called stanchions, these secure your girl's head, have a place for a feeder, and usually elevate her for a better milking height. See Chapter 7 Resources on page 214 for where to find DIY plans.

Cleanliness

Keeping the udder, equipment, and your hands ultra clean is key to good-quality milk. Animal hair and dander plus certain kinds of bacteria can taint the flavor of the milk. Most of the following points are common sense:

* Use only seamless stainless steel and glass for milk catching and storage. Seams in pails are difficult to clean and can harbor bacteria.

* Wash your hands in hot soapy water and dry thoroughly before milking.

* Wash and massage the entire udder with warm water to remove dirt, loose hair, and dander. Some people add a disinfectant to their washing water such as a few drops of bleach, iodine, vinegar, grapefruit essential oil, or dishwashing liquid.

* Use clean, unused cloths for each animal to be milked.

* Discard the first squirts of milk to clear the teat orifice of dirt and bacteria (your barn cat will appreciate these).

* Use a clean strainer and fresh filtering cloths to strain the milk.

* Clean equipment with fresh, hot, soapy water immediately after milking. Rinse with hot water and allow to air dry (towels and dishcloths may introduce bacteria).

* Boil reusable washing cloths and allow to air dry.

Milk Letdown

Your cow, doe, or ewe is completely in control of her milk. If she doesn't want to let it down, you won't get a drop! This is the reason for massaging while washing the udder: It stimulates her letdown reflex. It helps if your mood is calm, gentle, and patient. Some people find singing encourages letdown.

Hand Milking

Many times a novice will attempt to get milk by pulling on the teat. The result? Nothing. To get milk by hand we have to simulate the baby's sucking by squeezing it out. Hold your hand out flat, then bend first your index finger, then middle finger, then ring finger, and lastly

Hand milking a goat

the pinky. Repeat. The rhythm of this action squeezes milk out of the udder. This is easier to demonstrate than explain, so if you don't have someone with experience to show you, I've included links to videos in Resources.

Machine Milking

If you are milking sheep or a doe with short teats, or have arthritis, consider a milking machine. Most are heavy-duty, expensive, and geared toward commercial milk production; however, small, inexpensive milking machines do exist. The simplest is made from a wide-mouth jar, large veterinary syringes, food-grade vinyl tubing, and a manual brake bleeder. These can be bought premade with the option to milk one to four teats at a time, or you can make one yourself. See Chapter 7 Resources page 214 for links to both.

Disinfectants and teat dips or sprays are necessary with machine milking because the equipment can easily harbor bacteria. Clean yours according to manufacturer's directions.

Stripping

Stripping is the process of milking out every last drop. Milk production is based on demand, so stripping is something you must do, or the milk left in the udder will signal your girl's body that she doesn't need to produce as much. If you are milk sharing (see Managing the

Milk Supply), the offspring will take care of this for you. If you are machine milking, follow the manufacturer's instructions. Even though the name implies pinching and pulling, the action is actually the same squeezing motion as for hand milking.

Teat Dips and Sprays

Teat dips (or sprays) are disinfectants used after milking and are necessary in some circumstances. They are always used after machine milking to prevent mastitis. For hand milking, it depends. It takes 15 to 30 minutes for the teat orifice to close again after milking, so if there's a chance your girl will go lie down in the dirt before then, use one. If you would like to use something mild, a squirt to each teat with vinegar may be all you need. Bleach is sometimes recommended, but it is drying on the skin. Commercial products are also available (see Resources). If you are sharing the milk with the calves or kids, do not use a teat dip or spray unless you don't mind the baby ingesting it.

MANAGING THE MILK SUPPLY

Milk sharing with the calf, lambs, or kids is an excellent way to make your workload lighter. No formula to mix, no bottles to fill and clean, no need to work bottle feeding into your schedule. The beauty of milk sharing is not only less work for you, but if you ever need a break from milking or have to be away from the homestead, the milking will be taken care of for you.

Cows. For the first month, a cow will produce more milk than her calf can consume. During this time, you can milk her twice a day and the calf will still get plenty. At about four weeks old, your share will begin to decrease quite a bit. The calf will be eating some solid food by then, so you can separate the calf at night, milk in the morning, and let the calf have the milk for the rest of the day.

Goats and sheep. The routine is similar to the one for cows but with a different time frame. By about two weeks of age, kids and lambs are eating some hay and forage, so they can be separated at night for you to get the morning milk. I give my kids a pan with a little feed at night, and once they learn they'll get a special treat if they go into the stall, they are easy to separate from their dams. An alternative for sheep is to not start milking until after the lambs are weaned at about a month old.

If you want to have milk all year, the simplest way is to have two milking animals and offset their breeding and birthing dates.

Some goats will produce milk for longer than the typical 8 to 10 months. They are "milked through" the breeding season and continue to supply milk while the others are dry during their pregnancies. These individuals can be bred every two years or so. This is an individual trait, however, and won't be true of all does.

MILK PROCESSING

Straining

Strain immediately into spotlessly clean, dry glass jars. If you don't want to use reusable straining cloths, you can purchase milk filters or even use a coffee filter for small amounts. Date your jar, and if you are milking twice a day, add a.m. or p.m. to indicate morning or evening milking. Chill immediately.

Home Pasteurizing

Many people prefer raw milk, but you can easily pasteurize yours if you wish. Although conventional low-heat pasteurization will not increase the shelf life of your milk, it will give you peace of mind if you have concerns about drinking and using raw milk.

To pasteurize, heat your milk to one of the following for the recommended length of time:

- 145°F (63°C) for 30 minutes
- 161°F (72°C) for 15 seconds
- 191°F (89°C) for 1 second

Milk pasteurized at these temperatures is perfectly fine for cheese making, whereas commercial ultra-high temperature (UHT) pasteurized milk is not. UHT denatures milk protein molecules to increase shelf life; however, they will not coagulate to make cheese.

Please keep in mind that pasteurization is *not* a substitute for correct milk handling or maintaining cleanliness standards.

Keeping Production Records

It isn't necessary to keep a written record of how much milk you're getting unless you want to. I store my milk in ½-gallon canning jars, so I always know when I have enough for my next batch of cheese. If you have production, breeding, or promotion goals, however, you will likely want to keep records.

Milk is measured by weight, not volume, because although it is mostly water, it also contains milk solids and butterfat. The proportions of these vary not only by species but also by individual. That means that a gallon of milk from two different animals won't necessarily weigh the same.

To keep your own records, use a hanging scale calibrated to zero with your empty milking bucket attached. Weigh each individual's milk after milking and record the amount in pounds and ounces for that particular date. You can work out your totals and averages from that.

KEEPING MILK

Raw milk has natural antibacterial properties that deter putrefying microorganisms. Even so, raw milk will naturally sour as the native lactobacillus in the milk converts the milk sugars to lactic acid. The lactic acid continues to protect milk from spoiling, first making a natural yogurt-like product, and eventually separating into curds and whey (called clabber). Although few of us would care to drink a glass of sour milk, it is useful for baking, cooking, as a culture for making cheese, and to feed pigs, chickens, or pets.

Pasteurized milk will not so much sour as putrefy. When this happens, it is not safe to use and must be discarded.

Slowing the Souring of Milk

The natural souring of raw milk will happen quickly in warm temperatures and more slowly in cold temperatures. The recommended temperature for storing milk is 35 to 38°F (1.6 to 3.3°C) for the longest possible freshness. This is easily maintained with a refrigerator, but there are off-grid ways to keep milk cool. Just keep in mind that how quickly milk sours depends on the temperature at which it is stored. Always use the freshest milk for drinking and table use. With all storage methods, remember to date your jars and let your nose be your guide. If you are producing more sour milk than you need, gear production to no more than you can use in a day or two, or use it to feed other animals.

See Off-Grid Storage of Eggs, Milk, and Meat (page 153) for ways to keep milk cool without a refrigerator.

Uses for Soured or Clabbered Milk

So, what can you do with milk that has soured or clabbered?

Baking. Before the invention of baking powder, old recipes for baked goods called for soured or clabbered milk and saleratus (baking soda). Modern versions of these recipes often call for making your own sour milk by adding 1 tablespoon of vinegar or lemon juice per cup of milk and letting it stand for about five minutes. If you have raw milk that has soured naturally, you can use ½ teaspoon of baking soda per ½ cup sour milk.

Cheese. Soured raw milk is a perfect starter culture for making cheese. Add ½ cup per ½ gallon of fresh milk in place of other starters.

Animal feed. Pigs adore soured and clabbered milk. Feed it straight or mix it into their usual slop. Poultry, cats, and dogs may like it too, depending on their tastes. It should be noted that poultry lack the enzyme to digest lactose, the milk sugar in fresh milk. By the time milk has soured to the point of clabbering, the lactose has been converted to lactic acid. However, if your poultry develop diarrhea, stop giving them soured milk.

Dairy products. Strain the curds from the whey and use them as a yogurt, cream cheese, or sour cream substitute. You can use the whey in baking just as you can sour milk.

Off-Tasting Milk

Raw milk will sour naturally over time, but if your fresh milk tastes bitter right from the source or begins to sour after only a couple of days, there are ways to correct it. This is not an especially common problem, but it does happen. Listed below are possible causes and how to address them.

Cleanliness. The first step is to review your milking and milk-handling routine as detailed on page 129. If your methods are scrupulous and you still have a problem, try the following:

❁ Sterilize or scald your equipment and jars.

❁ Allow your hands and the udder to air dry.

❁ Launder reusable milk-straining and udder cloths well between uses. Do not let them sit in a damp pile, but let them dry completely. If you are still dealing with off-tasting milk, boil them. Remember to use a clean one for each animal, one per use.

Remember, pasteurization is not a substitute for cleanliness.

Chilling. The more quickly milk is chilled, the longer it will take to sour. Strain and chill milk immediately after milking. In summer, some people keep their jars in the freezer to help cool the milk more quickly. I have a large bucket that will hold my milking bucket plus an ice pack.

Milk storage. The best temperature for storage is 35 to 38°F (1.6 to 3.3°C). If you are unable to maintain this, then your experience will teach you how long it takes before your milk begins to sour.

Diet. Some plants will impart an off flavor to milk if eaten in large quantities. These include brassicas such as cabbage and turnips, and alliums such as onion and garlic. Some commercial feeds will change the flavor of milk. These may vary amongst individuals.

Minerals. A deficiency of B vitamins can cause off-tasting milk. This can be corrected with a yeast supplement, or by adding cobalt to your mineral mix.

Mastitis. This can change the flavor of milk. Severe mastitis can make milk undrinkable.

Buck near the does. Most people think this is always true, but it's just anecdotal. I've kept a buck with my does for months without any change in milk flavor, and other goat folk have said the same. That doesn't mean it can't happen, so when you're working through a checklist of things to correct milk flavor, try this as a last resort.

Genetics. Sometimes, no matter what you do, milk is off-flavored because that's how the individual produces it. The options are to cull her, or use her milk for other purposes such as feeding pigs and chickens (unless it's so bad even they reject it), or making soap.

BUTTER

Milk will naturally separate into milk and cream as it sits. Some people think goat's milk is naturally homogenized, but this isn't so.

Homogenized milk will never separate because the fat globules are mechanically processed and evenly disbursed in the milk. This is not the case with goat's milk. Goat's milk is simply slower to separate than cow's milk, because its fat globules are smaller, plus it lacks a particular protein that enables the fat globules in cow's milk to bond together more quickly. Let your goat milk sit for at least three days, and you will be able to skim the cream. The same is true for sheep's milk.

There are three ways in which you can collect the cream for butter.

* Hand skimming: After the cream is separated from the milk, you can remove it with a ladle or turkey baster.

* Spigot jars: Use these for your freshly strained milk instead of canning jars. Once the cream separates, open the spigot and remove the milk from the bottom.

* Cream separator: These can be either electric or manual and cost several hundred dollars. Best used for large amounts of milk. Follow the manufacturer's instructions to use.

Butter is made by agitating the cream in a butter churn, mixer, or blender, or by shaking in a jar. Temperature is key. If your cream is between 50 to 60°F (10 to 15°C), you should have good results. Warmer and your butter will melt, colder and you'll make whipped cream.

Washing butter. Once your butter has formed, pour off the buttermilk and put the butter in a bowl with cold water. "Wash" your butter by pressing out the excess buttermilk with a wooden spoon. Some people omit this step, but washed butter will keep longer. Churned buttermilk is not the same product that is sold in the grocery stores. That buttermilk has been cultured, whereas yours will be thin and "sweet." It's not a waste product, however, and is excellent for baking.

Storing butter. Currently there is a debate among experts as to whether or not butter needs to be refrigerated. The fat itself is fairly stable, but milk solids in the butter will sour. The shelf life of butter can be improved by washing and salting it. Salt is a flavor enhancer, but also a preservative. The following methods are good options for storing butter.

* Refrigerate or freeze for the longest storage. The colder it is, the longer it will keep. To freeze, use wax or freezer paper for best results. Defrost in the refrigerator.

* Clarify: Clarification removes milk solids from butter and is said to triple its shelf life. To clarify, gently melt and simmer in a saucepan. The foam that forms is the milk solids. Skim these off and use on popcorn or baked potatoes. Continue simmering and skimming until only a clear yellow liquid remains. Pour through a strainer into a jar.

* Ghee: This is clarified butter with a darker color and nutty flavor. To make it, melt as for clarified butter, but do not skim. The milk solids will sink to the bottom of the pan as it simmers and turn golden brown. Strain your ghee into a canning jar or other container.

* French butter keeper: This ceramic or pottery butter holder also keeps butter without refrigeration. It consists of two cup-shaped pieces, one fitting inside of the other. Butter is packed into the smaller of the two cups, and the larger is filled about a third full of lightly salted, cooled water. The butter cup is turned upside down and fits into the water cup. The water seals the butter so that it remains soft and fresh for each use.

CULTURED MILK: YOGURT AND KEFIR

Yogurt is a popular homemade milk product, but for the prepper minded, I'm going to recommend kefir instead. Both are cultured milk products which require the introduction of a starter. The difference is that yogurt starters require a specific heat and eventually wear out.

That means they must periodically be replaced. Kefir starter, known as grains, reproduces itself!

To make yogurt: Heat milk almost to a simmer and let cool to 110° to 115°F (43° to 46°C). Stir in 1 tablespoon of yogurt culture and maintain the same temperature until the milk thickens. Store in a cool place.

To make kefir: Mix 1 tablespoon kefir in a pint of milk. Let sit for 18 to 48 hours, or until it thickens. Strain out the grains, place them in fresh milk, and store your kefir in a cool place.

Both yogurt and strained kefir can be hung in a loose-weave fabric to drain the whey and make delightfully tangy, spreadable cheeses.

See Cultured Milk under Resources for where to find detailed information on both.

CHEESE

Cheese is the traditional way to preserve milk, but it's an extensive subject and beyond the scope of this handbook. For the prepper or those striving for sustainable cheesemaking, I highly recommend David Asher's *The Art of Natural Cheesemaking.* Sustainable substitutes for commercial starters (cultures) and milk additives follow.

If you are concerned about using raw milk in cheese, age the cheese for at least 60 days. This is the aging time required by the USDA for selling raw milk cheeses to the public.

Sustainable cultures. These can be substituted for commercial thermophilic and mesophilic starters. Commonly used are kefir, yogurt, whey, cultured buttermilk, and soured raw milk. In general, use ¼ to ½ cup per gallon of milk. If your cheese is too bland for your taste, increase the amount of culture in your next batch. If your cheese tastes too sour, decrease it.

Natural rennets. Animal rennets are made from the stomach of a calf or kid, where enzymes curdle liquid milk into soft, digestible curds. See "How to Make Calf or Kid Rennet" under Resources for how to make your own. Plant rennets are made from plants that will curdle milk: thistle, cardoon, ground ivy, sheep sorrel, butterwort leaves, mallow, yarrow, teasel, knapweed, perennial ryegrass, narrowleaf plantain, henbit, shepherd's purse, kudzu, globe artichoke, Jerusalem artichoke flowers, Irish moss, and safflower are examples.

To make the rennet, gather and dehydrate any of the above. Make a strong tea by boiling a handful of the plant matter in 2 cups of water. Use ½ cup of tea per ½ gallon of milk. Results may vary!

Fig sap. The white latex-like sap from figs will also curdle milk. It only takes a few drops per quart of milk, and makes a soft, spreadable cheese.

Calcium chloride. This is often recommended when using pasteurized milk for making cheese. In raw milk the calcium is correctly balanced, so calcium chloride is not necessary.

Preserving cheese. If cheese is a way to preserve milk, then how do we preserve cheese? Cheeses that aren't eaten fresh can be waxed, bandaged, or stored in oil or brine. The idea is to keep the cheese from becoming contaminated by airborne bacteria and fungi that might change your cheese in undesirable ways.

Waxing. The most common way to preserve cheese. Cheeses are coated with melted wax and then aged. Beeswax is an alternative to commercial cheese wax. If you find beeswax too brittle and prone to cracking, coconut oil or vegetable shortening can be added to melted beeswax to increase pliability:

* 13.5 ounces melted beeswax

* 2.5 ounces oil or shortening

Waxed cheeses are typically aged 60 days or longer at 50 to 60°F (10 to 15°C) and 75 to 95 percent humidity.

Bandaging. Another option for aging and storing cheese. Several layers of cotton cloth are cut in rounds for the top and bottom of the cheese wheel, and strips cut for the sides. The bandage is coated with butter or lard and then aged the same as waxed cheeses.

Oil submersion. Used for soft cheeses. The cheeses are submerged in extra-virgin olive oil and kept in a cool root cellar or refrigerator. Herbs such as rosemary, thyme, bay leaves, savory, oregano, peppercorns, and garlic may be added to the oil for flavoring. The herbed oil may later be used for salads and sautéing.

Brined cheeses. Common in areas where colder cave storage isn't traditionally available. Feta and mozzarella are two examples. To make the brine, use:

* 1 cup non-iodized salt

* 1 gallon whey

Submerge the cheese in the brine and store in a cool place.

Brined cheeses tend to get saltier the longer they are stored, but can be rinsed off with cool water before serving if desired.

Cold storage. Cold storage, such as a root cellar or cheese cave, can be used to store cheese without refrigeration.

* Cured, uncut cheeses can be stored until it's time to consume them.

* Cut cheeses will keep longest if kept as cold as possible. Cut off mold as it develops and feed it to the pigs, chickens, or compost. The rest of the cheese is still good.

* Natural rinded cheeses will need to be examined periodically for growth of molds. Moldy spots can be scrubbed with vinegar and salt to remove the mold.

* Waxed cheeses need to be turned about once a week to keep the natural moisture within the cheese from settling on the bottom.

✻ Brine- or oil-kept cheeses must be checked periodically to make sure they remain submerged.

Freezing. Generally not recommended for cheese, because freezing alters the texture and causes the cheese to be crumbly. It still has good flavor, however, and is acceptable for cooking. Some cheeses such as grated mozzarella and paneer, freeze very well.

MEAT

If you raise animals for meat, plan to harvest in autumn. Animals born in spring have grown and gained weight but are still young enough to be tender. Colder weather limits the possibility of spoilage and exposure to flies. Rabbit and poultry are the exception, because they grow quickly and are harvested by weight or age. For Dan and me, autumn is the time we take stock of our livestock numbers and availability of feed for the winter. Our goal is to keep a balance. Having to overwinter too many animals tips that balance.

General Considerations

Harvesting animals for meat is a two-step process: killing (slaughtering) and butchering. Killing may also be referred to as "dispatching," while butchering refers to cutting the carcass into various cuts of meat.

For large animals, the preferred temperature for processing is 35 to 40°F (1.6 to 4.4°C). Morning is a good time to begin, because it's a big job. For poultry, Dan and I plan to do the killing before sunrise. It's much easier to snatch a bird off the roost than to chase it around the chicken yard. We can handle five or six chickens within a couple of hours.

For your first time, I suggest assisting someone else with their animals. Nothing beats hands-on experience, especially if your mentor is willing to explain things to you and answer questions. Ask them to identify the organs, because the real thing rarely looks like the pictures in the book.

Don't rush. You are working with sharp instruments while learning a new skill, so work carefully. The meat won't go bad even if it takes you several hours to do the job.

To sell meat, facilities for both slaughtering and butchering must be government inspected and approved. Without certification, it is not legal for you to sell a slaughtered animal to someone else, nor is it legal to allow them to purchase an animal from you and kill it on your property.

Mental and Emotional Preparedness

Everything that follows is going to be seem matter-of-fact and emotionally sterile. The reality of harvesting your own meat is anything but! I'm not going to pretend it's easy the first time, or any time after that. My husband and I do it for the sake of our self-sufficiency goal, to prevent overpopulation of a particular species on our homestead, and because we believe we should take responsibility for the food we eat.

People will advise you to not become emotionally attached to animals you intend to eat, but that's not an easy task, especially when it's all new. They'll tell you not to name them or to give them names like "Hamburger" or "Pork Chop." We haven't found that to help. If you think you simply cannot do the deed but still want to raise your own meat, consider one of the following:

❋ Take the animal to a meat processor.

❋ Hire someone. In some areas, there are licensed mobile butchers who will do as little or as much of the process as you wish.

❋ Trade animals with someone wanting to do the same thing. It may be easier to process an animal you didn't raise yourself.

If you do decide to do it yourself, my best advice is to make the decision, set the date, and then systematically follow the checklist of things to do. Don't think about the animal or how you feel, just focus your full attention on each step, one at a time, and before you know it, it will be done and you'll have survived!

Typical Ages of Animals for Slaughter

The age at which to process an animal depends on a number of factors: best yield of tender meat, not wanting to feed over winter, overcrowding, or dealing with an aggressive animal that shouldn't be foisted off on someone else. Religious food customs may factor in as well; for example, Islamic Ramadan, Jewish Passover, and Christian Easter are traditional holidays for lamb or goat meat.

WHEN TO PROCESS LIVESTOCK

ANIMAL	TYPE OF BREED/MEAT	AGE OR WEIGHT
CATTLE Steers (castrated males) are usually preferred for meat.	Veal	1 to 3 months
	Beef	9 months
GOAT The terms cabrito and chevon are often used interchangeably, but cabrito is meat from a milk-fed kid.	Cabrito	4 to 8 weeks
	Chevon	6 months and older
SHEEP	Lamb	Before 12 months (18 months for wethers)
	Mutton	After 12 months (18 months for wethers)
PIGS (by weight)	Standard-size	200 to 225 pounds or larger
	American Guinea Hog	120 pounds
POULTRY These ages refer to heritage breeds, not faster-gaining hybrid meat birds	Chickens	By 8 months
	Turkey	6 to 8 months
	Guinea fowl	12 to 18 weeks

WHEN TO PROCESS LIVESTOCK

ANIMAL	TYPE OF BREED/MEAT	AGE OR WEIGHT
WATERFOWL Easiest to pluck if harvested when they have the fewest pin feathers. Older birds are good candidates for canning, pressure cooking, or slow cooking.	Ducks	7, 12½, or 18 weeks
	Geese	9, 15, or 20 weeks
RABBITS	Confined rabbits	8 weeks
	Pasture-raised rabbits	10 to 12 weeks

HOW MUCH MEAT CAN YOU EXPECT?

Some parts of an animal are inedible, such as hide, blood, feet, heads, and innards. This means there is a difference in body weights before and after processing; these are referred to as live and hanging weights. You can expect hanging weights to be approximately:

❊ Cattle: 60% of live weight

❊ Sheep and goats: 50% of live weight

❊ Pigs: 70% of live weight

❊ Poultry: 75% of live weight

❊ Rabbit: 50% of live weight

That means that a cow weighing 1,100 pounds alive will have a hanging weight of about 660 pounds.

Hanging weight (also called dressed weight) includes muscle, fat, and bone. Depending on length of aging, further trimming, and the cuts you choose, your actual meat yield (called cut, package, or take-home weight) will be roughly 65 to 75% of the hanging weight, less for boneless cuts. So that same cow with 660 pounds hanging weight will yield somewhere around 460 pounds of meat for cooking.

All of these are rough estimates and actual results may vary.

EQUIPMENT AND SUPPLIES

In a nutshell, the animal is killed, bled out, eviscerated, and skinned outdoors. The carcass is usually taken to an indoor area for cutting up. We've done it outdoors as well.

Good-quality equipment is a must for every step. For killing, you will need a 9 mm or .38 pistol, or .22 rifle, along with hollow point or soft point bullets. Alternatively, you'll need a captive bolt pistol or stun bolt gun (for stunning) and a very sharp knife (for sticking and bleeding out).

You'll also need the following:

* skinning knife
* butcher knife
* boning knife
* cleaver
* sharpening stone
* sharpening steel
* hand or power meat saw (bone saw)
* gambrel or singletree (a frame from which to hang the carcass for eviscerating and skinning)
* ropes

* come-along (a hand-operated winch commonly used for pulling wire to install fence; useful for hoisting a small carcass, like that of a goat, sheep, or calf, to working height)
* block and tackle, chain hoist, or windlass (serve the same purpose as a come-along, but can pull heavier loads, like a cow or a large hog)
* tree or heavy-duty tripod for hanging the carcass
* large table at a comfortable height for meat cutting

- buckets to hold meat, organs, fat for rendering
- buckets to hold anything you wish to discard (called offal)
- garden hose and running water
- warm water for hand washing
- old towels or rags for hand wiping, or latex gloves (optional)
- apron or smock

For poultry, you'll also need a killing cone and a large pot of hot water. For hog scraping (instead of skinning), you'll need a vat, drum, or tank large enough to scald the hog, as well as a hog scraper.

You will also need somewhere cold to hang and age the meat, a way to dispose of the offal, and whatever equipment will be required for your preferred methods of storage: freezing, canning, or dehydrating. Brining and smoking will require crocks for brining and a smoker or smokehouse for smoking. You will need a meat grinder and sausage stuffer for making ground meat and stuffed sausages.

Preparation

Day before:

- Gather equipment.
- Sharpen knives if needed. A razor-shape knife is more efficient than a dull one.
- Separate the animal the night before. Do not feed but give access to clean water. An animal with an empty stomach is easier to process.
- Choose a spot for your killing and bleeding out, preferably away from and out of sight of its herd or flock mates.
- Review the steps if you need to.

Day of:

- Wipe down a work table with hot soapy water and bleach.

- Lay out knives, buckets, and other equipment.

- Have your book or a checklist handy for reference.

- Keep your routine as normal as possible. Animals sense when something is off and may become nervous or skittish.

- Calmly lead them to the place you've chosen and tie them up.

- Speak softly and gently.

- Some people offer feed as a distraction.

THE PROCESS

Following is a general overview. I recommend that you invest in a book geared specifically toward butchering livestock and game for better detail.

1) Shooting or stunning.

- Cows: Imagine an "X" from the eyes to horns or horn buds.

- Goats and sheep: Because of their horns and thick skulls, these are more humanely shot from behind. Aim behind the poll (base of horns) toward the angle of the jaw.

- Pigs: Imagine an "X" from the eyes to ears.

- Poultry: Hang in a killing cone and cleanly cut through the throat and arteries. Alternatively, snap its neck.

- Rabbits: Stun with a hard blow right behind the ears and cut off its head. Alternatively, snap its neck.

2) Bleed out. Immediately after shooting or stunning, slit the animal's throat, making sure to cut both carotid arteries and jugular veins. Hang the animal head down and allow to bleed out.

3) Pluck or skin. This is done for poultry.

4) Eviscerate. Cut the carcass open along the underbelly and remove organs. If you are processing an intact male (not neutered), remove the testicles. If you wish to preserve the pelt, it can be skinned first.

5) Remove skin, feet, tail. Try to keep hair off the muscle, as it tends to impart a strong flavor or taint to the meat.

6) Hose the carcass down. Use cold water, inside and out. This will remove dirt and hair, plus help cool it down.

7) Dispose of offal. Some people put it in their compost. You can also feed it to your pigs or bury it. Be aware that other animals may dig up the remains, so bury deeply or cover with boards or a scrap of fencing weighted with rocks.

8) Age the carcass. The reason for aging is to improve tenderness. Soon after death chemical changes in the muscles cause them to stiffen (rigor mortis). Aging allows natural enzymes to relax the muscles. The carcass is hung from four to seven days (24 hours for poultry and rabbits) at 35°F (1.5°C). High humidity will help prevent drying out.

9) Make your meat cuts. There is no right or wrong here, just convention for the sake of labeling meat in the grocery store. Try to find the tendons in the joints and cut through these with a sharp knife. Use your meat or bone saw to cut through bones. Meat scraps can be used as stew meat or to make ground meat or sausage.

KEEPING MEAT

Refrigerating. Meat keeps best at temperatures below 40°F (4.4°C). See Off-Grid Storage of Eggs, Milk, and Meat (page 153) for more ideas.

Freezing. Raw meat should be wrapped tightly in freezer paper or plastic wrap. Some people vacuum seal it.

Canning. This is a great prepper way to preserve and store meat. It can be partially cooked or at least simmered until hot throughout. Cover with boiling water or broth and leave 1 inch of headspace. Process at 10 pounds pressure (adjusted for altitude)—75 minutes for pints, 90 minutes for quarts. For detailed instructions and recipes, I recommend Daisy Luther's *The Prepper's Canning Guide*.

Dehydrating. Because dehydrating is achieved through relatively low temperatures over hours, it is recommended that you only dehydrate cooked meat. This is important to kill any pathogens that will survive the dehydrator. Trim away as much fat as possible, because the fat will spoil before the meat will. Cut into ½-inch cubes or thin strips.

* Dehydrator: Dry at 140°F (60°C) for six hours. Turn meat and rotate trays, then set the dehydrator to 130°F (55°C) until thoroughly dry. The pieces should be hard.

* Sun: Spread in a single layer on a baking sheet. Place in the sun in an area that gets good ventilation. Turn over occasionally and bring in at night. Drying time will be two to three days, depending on the humidity.

* Oven: Spread in one layer on a baking sheet. Leave oven door ajar. Dry at 140°F (60°C) for six hours, then turn over and lower the temp to 130°F (55°C) until hard and dry.

* To rehydrate: Pour 1 cup of boiling water over 1 cup of dried meat and allow to sit for three to four hours. Or, simmer for half an hour.

For more detail and recipes, I recommend Phyllis Hobson's *Making & Using Dried Foods*.

Salting, brining, curing, smoking. The first time I saw country ham for sale in the grocery store I was quite surprised. It sat on display in the middle of the aisle—not refrigerated! This was quite shocking to my modern mind, but as I've studied prepper methods of food storage I've learned that salting, brining, curing, and smoking were common ways to preserve meat before the invention of refrigeration. The key is salt. Salt deters bacteria and draws out excess moisture, both of which are important for this method of preservation. There are many variations to these techniques, including:

* Salting and brining: Cut a raw pork roast into 1-pound pieces and layer with salt in a stoneware crock or wooden barrel. Cover with a brine solution of salt and water (strong enough to float a raw egg), weight the meat to submerge it, and store in a cool place. It will keep for months, but check it periodically. If the mixture bubbles, pour it off, rinse the meat, and cover with a fresh batch of brine.

* Curing and smoking: Cure mixtures contain salt, sugar (white or brown), pepper (red or black), and sometimes saltpeter. Rub dry onto raw meat. For large pieces, make cuts 1 to 2 inches deep, and rub in the cure mixture thoroughly. Place in an old pillow case or muslin bag, and hang in a cool place to air dry for several months. Then it can be smoked if desired. Hot smoking cooks the meat; cold smoking preserves the meat without cooking. See Meat Curing and Smoking in Resources for where to find more information.

To prepare salt-preserved meat for consumption, soak in fresh water for several hours to overnight. Change the water several times. Towel dry and cook the same as fresh meat.

Large cuts such as country hams sometimes grow mold on the surface. Cut this off and discard. As with mold on cheese, the meat underneath is still good to eat.

All meat preserved with these methods must be properly cooked. Use a meat thermometer to determine doneness.

Confit. This preservation technique comes to us from France. It refers to meat preserved in its own rendered fat. Traditionally this is done with duck and goose, but pork or other meats may be used too.

Salt and season the meat heavily and allow to sit several hours. Wash off and pat dry. Heat the rendered fat to 200°F (90°C) and submerge the meat in it. (See Meat Byproducts below for how to render fat.) Cook for two to three hours or until tender. To store, place meat pieces in a stoneware crock and cover with melted fat. In a cool place, it is said to keep for months.

Mincemeat. Mincemeat recipes date back to the days of the Crusades. Cooked mutton, beef, goose, venison, or tongue is mixed with suet (pure white fat found around the kidneys), vinegar or lemon juice, sugar, dried fruits, and spirits. It is aged at least several weeks, and then baked in crusts as pies. The sugar, vinegar or lemon juice, and spirits preserve the mixture, which can keep up to one year in a cold cellar or refrigerator. Mincemeat is a delicious option for preserving leftovers from a roast.

To preserve, the mincemeat is potted or tightly packed in a sterile jar or stoneware crock. Cut a piece of brown paper to fit the opening, press it down snugly on top of the contents, and top with about a cup of brandy. Cover the jar and store in a cool place. Mincemeat should age for two weeks, and will keep up to one year.

MEAT BYPRODUCTS

Bones, hooves, and poultry feet can be fed to dogs or cats on a raw meaty bone diet. Or they can be used to make a mineral- and gelatin-rich broth for soups, stews, gravies, or cooking grains. Place bones and scrubbed hooves and poultry feet in a large stockpot. Cover with water and add onions, carrots, celery, etc., if desired. Add ½ cup of vinegar and simmer slowly. The vinegar dissolves the minerals from the bones. Strain and freeze or can at 10 pounds pressure (adjusted for altitude), 20 minutes for pints, 25 minutes for quarts. The cooked veggies and bits of leftover meat can be added to soup or another dish.

Fat can be rendered for cooking. Rendering is the process of melting and pouring off animal fat to make lard or tallow. Cut the fat into small pieces and place in a large cast-iron Dutch oven. Cover the bottom with water and heat slowly. The water will simmer off and prevent the fat from browning before it melts. Strain into jars and cool. The leftover bits are the cracklings; eat as a snack or add to cornbread or scrambled eggs.

Small intestines are traditionally used as sausage casings. First squeeze out contents, and then rinse out with running water from a faucet or garden hose. Turn inside out and gently scrape clean.

Hides can be tanned for leather.

Pelts can be treated and used for rugs, wall coverings, or warm clothing. See Resources for where to find information on treating hides and pelts.

Organ meats can be cooked and eaten as is, used in sausages and scrapple, or fed to pets or omnivorous livestock (pigs and poultry).

OFF-GRID STORAGE OF EGGS, MILK, AND MEAT

None of the following methods come close to refrigeration for keeping power, but they will be cooler than your kitchen on a warm day. How long your eggs, milk, and meat stay fresh will depend on the temperatures you can attain, so keep your eye on them to check for spoilage.

Spring house. These were once common features on many farms. Cold spring water was channeled through these structures, and milk containers, for example, were stored in the water. If you have a cold spring on your property, such a structure might be a possibility for you too. I've also seen a spring-chilled cooler made from an old chest freezer. Cold spring water was piped into the freezer from upstream with an overflow outlet at the other end.

Root cellar. This once-common structure is usually found in the basement (cellar) or dug into a hillside. The goal is to aim for temperatures below 40°F (4.4°C) and above freezing, although this won't be consistent throughout the

Root cellar

structure. The temperature will be colder near the floor and warmer near the ceiling, so you can store items accordingly.

Ice house. If you live where your lakes freeze long and hard, you can collect the ice in blocks and use them to keep perishable foods cold. Store ice blocks in an insulated building, or use straw bales to make an affordable, temporary ice house. Pack the ice blocks in sawdust to slow melting.

Dug well. If you have an old-fashioned well with a shaft large enough to lower a bucket into, you can take advantage of the earth's cooler temperatures for keeping perishable items. Place them in a bucket, basket, or box, lower it into the well above water level, and tie it off.

Zeer pot (evaporative refrigerator). If you live in an area with low humidity, a zeer pot is useful for storing eggs, butter, and vegetables. A simple zeer pot can be made from two crocks or earthenware containers, one small enough to fit loosely inside the other. The space between is filled with sand, which is kept damp. Because evaporation decreases temperature, food in the zeer pot is cooled as the sand dries out. The exact amount of cooling depends on the relative humidity. Keep the sand damp and check contents frequently for freshness.

Cold shafts. Like the zeer pot, these work best in areas with low relative humidity. The cold shaft extends from crawl space to attic, where the temperature difference between the two draws cool air up through the shaft. It should be well-insulated and located away from exterior walls, with screens at top and bottom to protect the interior from rodents. Wire shelving holds food items inside the shaft. A well-insulated door allows access.

Solar-powered pantry. If going whole-house solar isn't an option, consider a small solar energy system, just enough to run a refrigerator and freezer. Another option would be using DC (direct current) refrigerators and freezers, such as those used in RVs. I highly recommend *Prepper's Total Grid Failure Handbook* by Alan and Arlene Fiebig for an easy, economical way to set up such a system.

CHAPTER 8

KEEPING THEM HEALTHY

Healthy animals are happy animals. They are alert, bright-eyed, and interested in their surroundings. They have shiny coats or feathers, good appetites, and are in good condition (neither too thin nor overweight). Animals that are properly fed and cared for have the best chance of living long, productive lives.

Spend time every day observing and getting to know your animals. If you know their normal movements and behaviors, you can quickly identify anything out of the ordinary.

Much of what we've discussed in this book is the foundation for good livestock health:

❋ Start with healthy, disease-free stock (Chapter 2).

❋ Provide good shelter with adequate space (Chapter 3).

❋ Feed the right diet with proper nutrition (Chapter 4).

❋ Provide proper care during breeding and pregnancy (Chapter 5).

❋ Provide good care during labor and delivery (Chapter 6).

❋ Take good care of newborns (Chapter 6).

❋ Keep them safe (coming in Chapter 9).

In this chapter, I will discuss routine care, prevention of problems, how to identify when something is wrong, and when you might need a veterinarian's help. There are a number of things you will need to have on hand, but rather than give you one overwhelmingly long list, I have broken it down into several shorter lists: basic supplies for routine care, a first aid kit, things you need to administer medications, and a list of medications you may wish to keep on hand. Also, see the Birthing Supplies chart on page 103.

The kinds of treatments and medications you choose to use will depend upon your health philosophy and the availability of resources.

Conventional treatments use chemicals and pharmaceuticals. These are utilized by most veterinarians, and information on them is readily available.

Natural, alternative, or organic treatments rely on herbs, homeopathic remedies, and essential oils. These are becoming increasingly popular but are still less common, so information on treatments is harder to find. See Resources for how to find a holistic, homeopathic, or alternative medicine vet.

You'll need some basic supplies for routine care:

❋ Grooming brushes

❋ Halter and lead

❋ Hoof trimmers, rasp, and pick

❋ Styptic powder, an antiseptic powder to stop bleeding

❋ Toenail clippers

❋ Sheep shears and sharpener, if you plan to do your own shearing

❋ Large towel

In addition, I recommend a stethoscope for checking vital signs and a veterinary rectal thermometer. Although you won't use these last two items regularly, it's a good idea to have them on hand before you need them.

GROOMING

Animals love being petted, scratched, and groomed. Routine grooming is done with a brush to remove loose hair and smooth the fur. It offers an opportunity to check the animal over for scratches, wounds, lumps, bumps, or skin conditions that might be hidden by fur. Regular handling keeps animals tame and makes it easier to do examinations or other procedures.

SHEARING

Wool-producing sheep require regular shearing. Typically, this is done before spring lambing. A fleece harvested at this time of year is cleaner and produces good-quality fiber. In addition, you will be able to observe the ewe during labor and delivery, plus it gives the lambs easier access to their mother's milk.

An experienced shearer can remove the entire fleece with one pass of the shears. Shearing is something of a lost art, however, so if you can't find someone to hire for the job, you will need to learn the skill yourself. Shears are expensive, but good ones are worth the investment, especially if you consider that having the skill can earn you extra income. Contact your state agricultural department for possible shearing schools near you.

Shearing sheep

HOOF AND FOOT CARE

Almost all livestock need foot care, even if only occasionally. You will need a helper, head gate, or halter and lead to restrain the animal. This is a skill best learned by demonstration, so ask your mentor or vet to show you how, or find a good DVD on hoof trimming. Keep styptic powder handy in case you trim too close. The powder will help stop the bleeding.

Cows, sheep, and goats will need their hooves trimmed routinely unless they wear them down on rocky ground. The toe grows fastest and causes foot and posture problems if it gets too long. Extra growth is trimmed off and the toe trimmed back.

Pigs occasionally need their hooves trimmed, especially if they are confined to soft surfaces. When the nail starts to curl, it's time for a trim.

Rabbits need nail trimming. Pet nail clippers or human toenail clippers work well. Bundle your bunny in a towel and trim one foot at a time.

Poultry shouldn't need claw trimming unless they are caged. If they are free to scratch the ground, their nails will wear naturally.

VACCINATIONS

These may also be part of your routine care. Check with your veterinarian or mentor for which ones to use in your location. Most are optional but some are required by law. Your options include:

Conventional. These are injected and will vary according to species and your area. Most are over-the-counter and available at your local feed store or mail-order livestock supply.

Alternative. Includes working toward natural resistance and keeping a closed herd. A closed herd has had all animals previously quarantined for a minimum of 30 days for observation, worming, and testing before being released into the herd. No stud services are offered or used, and visitors are often restricted.

Homeopathic. In homeopathy, nosodes replace vaccines. Given orally, they are prepared from infected sources to cause the recipient to develop its own immune response to the disease.

INTEGRATED PARASITE MANAGEMENT

All species of animals are susceptible to internal parasites. These include parasitic worms and the coccidia protozoa. Fecal examinations of manure will reveal which particular parasites are present and how many. Most adults can tolerate a low parasite load, and your veterinarian may not treat until the fecal count gets to a certain level. An overload of parasites will kill animals, but you can prevent or minimize serious problems with proactive management techniques.

Worms

Prevention

The following are key considerations for preventing worms.

* Frequent pasture rotation: The typical life cycle for parasites is about 21 days, with larvae living for several days outside a host. Eggs can remain dormant for weeks or months.

* Rotation management: Rotate cattle with goats and sheep, as they pick up different parasites.

* Grazing management: Parasite eggs are dropped with manure, hatch on the ground, and travel 3 or 4 inches up wet or dewy forage. Rotate animals to another pasture before forage is grazed too short.

* Forage management: Include plants in your forage areas or hedgerows that promote worm resistance. Sericea lespedeza, birdsfoot trefoil, sainfoin, and chicory are four such plants.

* Good health with proper nutrition promote parasite resistance.

* Avoid stress. Parasites flourish in a stressed or sick animal.

* Breed for resistance. Cull individuals with consistently high worm loads.

* Don't use chemical wormers routinely or arbitrarily. This is how parasites develop resistance to wormers. Always base your decision to use a chemical wormer on a fecal test. You can have your vet do it for you, or purchase a microscope and kit to do your own. (See Do It Yourself Fecal Parasite Counts in Resources.)

Conventional Treatment

Chemical wormers are identified by class. Their effectiveness is dependent on whether there is resistance to the chemical or not. Your veterinarian will be able to tell you which classes of wormers still work in your area. Dosage is by the animal's weight. Administer according to the manufacturer's or your vet's instructions.

When used on milk or meat animals, there is a waiting ("withdrawal") period required before the milk or meat of the animal can be used. Follow the manufacturer's guidelines.

Alternative Treatment

Herbs, diatomaceous earth, garlic, and essential oils are often used, with no withdrawal period necessary. People debate their effectiveness, however, and a number of factors influence this: freshness, growing and harvest conditions, and processing methods. Dosage recommendations vary widely, as do reports of success. But as with any natural protocol, other factors have significant impact. For example, I live in a warm, humid climate which enables intestinal worms to thrive, while fellow goat breeders in arid areas report very few problems with parasites. I find I need higher doses more frequently than they do.

The following information will give you an idea of what it takes to naturally treat your livestock for parasites. I recommend that you have fecal exams done until you determine what works best for you. I also recommend investing in some of the books listed in Resources: Books for Your Homestead Library.

Important: For all worm treatments, conventional and alternative, the *only* way to determine effectiveness is with a fecal test. *Always* do a follow-up fecal exam two weeks after administering any wormer.

Herbs. There are numerous premixed herbal wormers available, plus lots of recipes around the internet to make your own. Commonly used herbs are wormwood, black walnut hull, garlic, oregano, thyme, cayenne, and pumpkin seeds, plus any number of other herbs for flavoring or nutritional support.

For cut and sifted herbs, give the initial dose once a day (twice a day for heavy worm load) for three to five days. For powdered herbs, give half the amount. For maintenance, provide the recommended dose once a week:

Cattle: 4 tablespoons

Goats: 1 tablespoon (kids under 2 months: ½ tablespoon)

Pigs: 2 to 3 teaspoons

Poultry: 1 tablespoon for every 6 chickens

Rabbits: ¼ teaspoon

Sheep: 2 teaspoons

Diatomaceous earth (D.E.). D.E. is also popular used alone, in an herbal formula, or added to loose minerals. Use food grade only.

Add D.E. to feed or offer free choice mixed with salt. Use one part D.E. to three parts salt. Administer for 21 days for intestinal parasites, 30 to 45 days for tapeworm, 90 days for lung worms. Here are the recommended daily dose of D.E. for deworming:

Cattle: 2% of dry feed ration and free choice

Poultry: 5% of dry feed ration plus free choice

Goats: 2 to 3 tablespoons per 100 pounds of body weight and free choice

Rabbits: ½ teaspoon per adult rabbit

Sheep: 2 to 3 tablespoons per 100 pounds of body weight and free choice

Pigs: 2% of dry feed ration and free choice

Garlic. Garlic can be fed fresh, as granules, powdered, juiced, tinctured, or as essential oil. It can be mixed with molasses to increase palatability.

Initially, give garlic daily for three to five days;, afterward, once a month, more frequently if your parasite problem persists. Fresh cloves can be fed as bulbs or whole plants. I feed one whole bulb to each of my goats monthly, chopped and sprinkled with molasses. For a cow, I might start with four bulbs.

Granules: Topdress regular feed ration every four weeks (cattle: 1 ounce per 1,000 pounds live weight; sheep and goats: ½ teaspoon per day for four to five days)

Powder: 1 ounce per 500 pounds live weight

Juice: 1 to 2 teaspoons per 200 pounds live weight

Tincture: 20 drops per day per 10 kilograms (22 pounds) live weight

Essential oils. Commonly used essential oils are oregano, thyme, lemongrass, and eucalyptus. Add to 3 cc olive or coconut oil. Give orally with dosing syringe for three days.

Large animals: add 2 to 3 drops each per 100 pounds body weight.

Small animals: add 1 drop each.

Rabbits: Use grapefruit seed oil, 10 drops per gallon of water for 2 weeks or longer if needed.

Coccidiosis

Coccidia are species-specific protozoa which thrive in warm, damp weather. An infection can be deadly for young animals and birds before they develop natural resistance, or for older animals in deteriorated health. Coccidia pass through a host's manure, so anywhere manure is deposited is a potential infection site. Early symptoms include appetite loss, listlessness, and hunched stance. Bloody diarrhea occurs in advanced infection. Dehydration from the diarrhea is usually the cause of death.

Prevention

Prevention includes the same treatment as for worms (page 160), plus:

* Keeping bedding clean

* Cleaning and disinfecting birthing areas

* Rotating farrowing locations

* Discarding dirty drinking water

* Keeping water buckets and waterers clean; disinfect if you find manure in them

* Not feeding animals off the ground

If you have an animal with symptoms, isolate it and have a fecal examination done to verify the problem.

Conventional Treatment

Products vary according to species but will be readily available from your feed store or mail-order supplier. Follow dosages on the label. Any species not listed on the label is considered "off label" for usage, which means the product was not tested for effectiveness on those animals. Check with your vet for instructions and dosage for off-label use.

Alternative Treatment

Herbs. Most herbal formulae are used for both worms and coccidia. Use the same dosage as listed in treatment for worms.

Garlic. Follow recommended dosage for worming.

Essential oil. Oregano has proven effective.

* Large animals: 2 to 3 drops in 3 cc olive or coconut oil per 100 pounds, once or twice daily for three to five days.

* Small animals: 1 drop in 2 to 3 cc olive or coconut oil per 20 pounds, once or twice daily for three to five days.

External Parasites

These can be a problem as well, with lice being the main culprit. Lice can be either biting or sucking, and both are contagious. Some kinds of lice cause mange.

Prevention. Provide quality forage and minerals, avoid close confinement, don't overcrowd, keep animals outdoors as much as possible, keep environment stress free.

Symptoms. Rough coat, shaggy appearance, excessive licking or rubbing, hair loss, bald patches, poor appetite, weight loss.

Conventional Treatment. Numerous topical products are available. Follow directions on the label.

Alternative Treatment. All are rubbed into the fur or feathers.

* Sulfur and/or diatomaceous earth (equal parts).

* Essential oils, such as camphor, eucalyptus, or rosemary. Use 1 part EO to 2 to 3 parts carrier oil (any vegetable oil will do).

NUTRITIONAL BALANCE

A number of livestock problems are feed and mineral related. The following lists describe common symptoms associated with deficiencies.

Mineral Deficiencies and Imbalance

Mineral supplements are recommended for livestock; however, it's important to understand that these only address their basic health requirements. If feed, forage, or hay lack specific minerals, it points toward soil deficiencies, which commercial supplements won't make up for. The US Geological Survey website (www.usgs.gov) offers soil mineral maps by county. It can give you an idea of soil deficiencies in your area. For specific data, you can have both soil and forage analyzed by a laboratory. Both tests are recommended, because if soil minerals aren't balanced the plants may not properly take up the minerals. Common mineral deficiencies in livestock are copper, selenium, cobalt, and iodine.

One of the most common mineral imbalances is the calcium-to-phosphorous ratio in the diet. An imbalance commonly occurs with a diet high in phosphorous-rich grains, and low in calcium-rich legumes. The most common problems are acidosis, milk fever, and urinary calculi (water belly). These can be avoided with a calcium-to-phosphorous ratio of two to one in the total diet. Legumes such as alfalfa are rich in calcium, or you can top-dress feed with dolomite powder or ground limestone.

Listed below are common symptoms of mineral deficiencies. The immediate solution to a deficiency is to offer specific minerals free choice. The long-term solution is to address deficiencies with specific soil amendments as recommended by your soil analysis.

Boron: Symptoms are joint problems, stiff gait, and creaking joints.

Calcium: Deficiencies are common in high-grain diets. Symptoms include bone and joint deformities, slow skeletal growth in young, weak and brittle bones, urinary calculi, or water belly (see page 171 for a detailed description of water belly), thin eggshells in poultry, muscular weakness, weak contractions during labor, milk fever in milk-producing animals (see Chapters 5 and 6), and mastitis.

Cobalt: This mineral is necessary for production of vitamin B12. Signs of deficiencies include loss of appetite, low weight gain, poor body condition, diarrhea (scours), rough and discolored hair coat, pale mucous membranes (anemia), runny eyes, staggering gait, bone deformities and fractures, decreased fertility, and mastitis.

Copper: Signs of deficiencies are dull rough coat, faded coat often starting around the eyes, reddish cast to hair color, infertility or reduced conception, anemia, increased susceptibility to internal parasites, reduced immune function, diarrhea in cattle, partial hind paralysis in pigs, loss of wool in sheep, and swayback in lambs.

Note: Requirements vary by species and too much copper can be toxic. If you practice multispecies grazing, it's a good idea to offer separate feeding areas with species-specific mineral feeders.

Iodine: Lack of iodine shows in swollen thyroid gland (goiter), hairless newborns, listlessness, impaired fertility, slow growth rate, and retained placenta.

Iron: Symptoms of iron deficiency are anemia, pale mucous membranes, listlessness, poor appetite, reduced milk production, and reduced growth rate. Iron deficiency is commonly seen in piglets and any animal with a heavy internal parasite load.

Manganese: This deficiency is often associated with a diet high in corn, because corn is low in manganese. Symptoms include weak joints and legs, poor conception rate, small ovaries and testicles, deformed newborns, calves born with contracted tendons, weakness and poor balance in pigs, and poultry developing enlarged hocks and having trouble moving.

Magnesium: Symptoms of low magnesium are tetany, nervousness, muscular twitching, excitability, poor bone development, reduced butterfat in the milk of dairy animals, hair loss, and excessive saliva.

Phosphorous: Deficiencies are common in high-legume diets. Symptoms include weak and brittle bones, infertility, retarded growth, loss of appetite, and pica (gnawing wood, rocks, or soil).

Potassium: Deficiencies are common in high-grain diets. Look for these symptoms: poor appetite, poor milk production, muscular weakness, weight loss, and lethargy.

Selenium: Deficiencies show up as white muscle disease in calves, lambs, and kids, poor growth rate, reduced conception rates, infertility, poor wool production in sheep, weakened immune system, susceptibility to infection, and high incidence of retained placenta. Selenium requires vitamin E to be assimilated.

Sulphur: Lice infestations.

Zinc: Low zinc symptoms are rough hair coat, stiff joints, swollen feet, hair and feather loss, itchy skin, flaky skin, scaly skin lesions, itching, and delayed wound healing.

Vitamin Deficiencies

Vitamin A: Deficiencies are often seasonal and occur in winter when no fresh forage is available, or when the diet is high in corn stalks. Symptoms include watery eyes, night blindness, rough coats in ruminants, posterior paralysis in young pigs, and reduced egg production for poultry.

Vitamin B1 (thiamine): This deficiency can result from sudden changes in diet or diets high in grain. Sypmtoms include stargazing (holding head up as if gazing at the stars), head rubbing, scours, weight loss, wasted appearance, goat polio.

Vitamin B2: Low vitamin B2 can be a problem for poultry (curled toe paralysis in chicks and reduced egg production in hens), and pigs (hairless piglets and skin lesions on adults).

Niacin: Deficiency is seen in high-grain diets, especially corn, which is low in niacin. Symptoms in pigs include poor growth, diarrhea, and dermatitis. In poultry, symptoms will be poor feathering and leg problems.

Vitamin B6: This deficiency is rarely a problem except when diets are high in flax seed (linseed) meal. Symptoms will include skin and reproductive problems.

Pantothenic acid: Deficiencies are most commonly seen in pigs and poultry, where the diet is high in corn or sorghum (milo). Poultry exhibit retarded growth, feather loss, and possible neurological symptoms. In pigs, a goose-stepping gait may be present.

Biotin: Deficiencies may occur in poultry on wheat-based diets. Symptoms include loss of feathers, cracks in skin on feet, and poor reproduction.

Vitamin B12: Vitamin B12 is synthesized in the rumen if adequate cobalt is available in ruminants' diets. A deficiency will result in a bitter flavor to milk. In poultry and pigs, a B12 deficiency will result in slow growth, anemia, poor reproduction, and hatching problems for chicks.

Vitamin C: Manufactured by almost all livestock, vitamin C shortages are rare unless the animal is under great stress.

Vitamin D: Vitamin D deficiency is rare in pastured animals, which receive sunlight. Problems include bone formation and soft egg shells.

Vitamin E: Vitamin E is important for assimilation of selenium. Symptoms include white muscle disease in young ruminants, retained placenta, and low fertility.

Vitamin K: Vitamin K is synthesized in the rumen, but supplementation may be necessary if your stock is grazing sweet clover, or for pigs and poultry battling coccidiosis. A deficiency increases bleeding and slows clotting time.

Proper diet plus a good-quality vitamin and mineral supplement is your best plan for prevention. For making your own herbal vitamin and mineral mix, see Minerals and Vitamins in Chapter 4.

OTHER PREVENTABLE PROBLEMS

Also see Diet-Related Problems on page 110.

Acidosis

Also called grain overload or grain poisoning, acidosis is a problem in ruminants fed a high-grain diet. The rumen is designed for the slow digestion of high-cellulose roughage, but grain contains easily digested carbohydrates. It ferments and becomes increasingly acidic until it compromises first the digestive, and then the immune system.

Symptoms: Loss of appetite, diarrhea, poor body condition, weight loss, lethargy, and elevated vital signs. Hoof problems can develop and the animal will eventually die.

Treatment: Reduce grain, offer long-stemmed roughage. Prevention is the best treatment.

Prevention: Feed primarily long-stemmed hay and pasture forage with minimal grain. Make gradual adjustments in feed to let ruminal microbes adjust. When turning onto new pasture, limit grazing to 15 minutes the first day, then gradually increase grazing time. Some folks leave baking soda in a mineral feeder for animals to self-treat.

Bloat

This problem affects ruminants who have a drastic change in diet. Perhaps they manage to break into the feed bin and gorge themselves, or overeat fresh green pasture before digestive microbes can adjust. The problem is excessive gas, which causes the belly to swell and bloat. If not treated immediately, it can be a killer.

Symptoms: Tight, overextended belly, obvious discomfort, collapse.

Treatment for cattle: Insert a stomach tube to relieve the gas.

Treatment for goats and sheep: Administer a mineral oil drench of 1 cup for adults, ¼ to ½ cup for kids or lambs.

Give probiotics once the symptoms are relieved.

Prevention: Avoid sudden changes in feed, especially increased amounts of grain. Restrict access to fresh, wet, or dewy green pasture.

Urinary Calculi (Water Belly)

This is another metabolic condition that primarily affects bulls, bucks, and rams. When the diet contains too much phosphorous (grain) with insufficient calcium (legumes), phosphatic crystals form in the bladder and get lodged in the urethra. These stones block urine from passing. If left untreated, the bladder will eventually rupture and the animal will die.

Symptoms: Restlessness, frequent attempts to urinate with little or no urine excreted, vocalizing when trying to urinate, tail twitching, stamping, teeth grinding (a symptom of pain), hunched posture when trying to urinate, swelling of the penis area, and swelling of the abdomen.

Treatment: Contact your veterinarian immediately! There are few options short of surgery, which has limited success.

Prevention: Proper diet is key. It must contain 2 to 2½ parts calcium to 1 part phosphorous. Calcium can be provided in alfalfa or other legumes, or by top-dressing feed with dolomite powder or ground limestone plus powdered vitamin C. Provide clean water at all times. Encourage drinking by increasing salt in the diet. People who choose to feed high-grain diets usually add ammonium chloride or apple cider vinegar to the water bucket to help acidify the urine to dissolve bladder crystals. Apple cider vinegar can also be sprayed onto feed (about a teaspoon per day).

Mastitis

Mastitis is an inflammation of the udder. All mammals are susceptible, but it's especially a concern with dairy animals. The cause is usually an infection resulting from sloppy milking habits or an injury, but genetics and diet are factors too. There are several kinds of mastitis, and early detection allows for the best treatment success. With subclinical mastitis, there are no symptoms, so it's helpful to routinely test your milkers. Inexpensive home detection tests are available, such as the California Mastitis Test or Dr. Naylor Mastitis Indicators.

Symptoms: Udder is hard, swollen, red, and may be lumpy and hot to the touch. Loss of appetite. She may flinch or kick when you touch her udder. Small clumps of milk may be passed, or it may contain blood and pus.

Conventional treatment: There are over-the-counter medications that can be squirted directly into the teat. Antibiotic injections will fight the infection systemically. Milk is the medium in which the bacteria thrive, so massage the udder and thoroughly milk out often.

Alternative treatment: Keep the udder completely milked out; strip three to six times per day to remove bacteria. Massage udder with essential oils of peppermint, tea tree, and oregano in a carrier oil. A poultice or salve of comfrey and poke root is very effective.

Dose the mother with her own infected milk. The mother passes the antibodies her body makes to her young through the milk. Her milk will contain the antibodies fighting the infection.

Boost the immune system by feeding garlic, vitamins A and C, aloe vera, kelp, and probiotics. Several herbal and homeopathic remedies can be useful as well. In Resources, see the link to the Ecological Agriculture Projects article "Treating Mastitis Without Antibiotics."

Prevention: Apply strict sanitation in your milking routine, especially if you use a milking machine. Use clean rags for washing and drying, one per animal. Use teat dips or sprays before and after milking. Don't let your milker lie down for at least 30 minutes after milking. This allows the teat orifice to close.

Nutritional Considerations

* Nonprotein nitrogens (NPNs) such as urea are linked to mastitis. If you purchase feed, check ingredient labels and avoid these.

* Milkers fed high-concentrate diets (feed pellets, grains, etc.) have a higher incidence of mastitis.

* Hypocalcemia promotes mastitis.

* Cobalt deficiencies have been linked to mastitis.

* Adequate selenium and vitamin E work together to reinforce the immune system to prevent mastitis.

* Homeopathic nosodes (prepared from infected sources to cause the recipient to develop its own immune response to infection) can be used to immunize the entire herd.

* Some animals are naturally more susceptible to mastitis than others. These may be candidates for culling.

WOUND AND ACCIDENT CARE

Accidents happen, as the saying goes. In addition to your general supplies, it's a good idea to put together a first aid kit containing these supplies:

- Antibacterial soap or scrub
- Antibacterial ointment
- Bandaging
- Adhesive tape
- Cotton balls, pads, and rolls for wound cleansing and padding
- Gauze nonstick pads
- Gauze rolls
- Self-stick bandage wrap such as Vet Wrap
- Betadine for wound cleansing
- Bleach for sterilizing equipment (also used to wipe tops of medicine bottles)
- Gloves, disposable latex or surgical
- Grooming clippers for shaving around wounds (also used for blood draw sites)
- Hydrogen peroxide, for flushing and cleaning wounds
- Paint stirrers, small and large, for setting fractures and stabilizing sprains
- Scissors, blunt nose or surgical
- Tweezers

OTHER MEDICATIONS

Medications are given as liquid drenches, gels, pastes, tablets, capsules, or injections. To administer these, you'll need:

* Drenching gun and/or dosing syringes for administering oral medications:

  » 6 to 15 cc for small animals

  » 20 to 60 cc for medium-size adults

  » 150 cc for cattle or dosing of multiple goats, sheep, or pigs

* Needles for measuring and administering vaccines and injectable medications. (Larger numbers indicate smaller gauges.)

  » Cattle: 16 and 18 gauge; 1- and 1.5-inch lengths

  » Goats and sheep: 18 and 20 gauge; 0.5-, 0.75-, and 1-inch lengths

  » Pigs: 16 and 18 gauge; 1- and 1.5-inch lengths

  » Kids, lambs, and piglets: 20 gauge; 0.5- and 1-inch lengths

  » Rabbits: 22 to 27 gauge; 0.5-inch length

  » Poultry: 20 to 25 gauge; 0.5-inch length

* Syringes for measuring and administering vaccines and injectable medications in 3 cc, 6cc, 12cc, 20cc, and 60 cc sizes.

  » Luer Lock syringes for injections. These have threaded tips to secure the needle by twisting it onto the syringe.

  » Luer Slip or catheter-tip syringes for oral medications.

To dispose of the syringe and needle, use containers such as a Sharps Container or an empty bleach bottle or milk jug. Ask your veterinarian or county health department for acceptable disposal sites.

Note that veterinary-grade needles and syringes are legal to purchase over the counter in most states, but in others it's by prescription only. Check with your veterinarian or county agricultural office for more information.

The following are good items to keep on hand for routine care or emergency treatments. Ask for your veterinarian's input. If you have an emergency, he or she can instruct you on what to administer while they are on their way.

Antibiotics

Antibiotics are used to treat bacterial infections and diseases and are commonly given by injection or added to the stock's drinking water. Follow the dosages listed on the labels or consult your veterinarian.

Conventional: Veterinary-grade antibiotics are available without prescription from most feed stores and mail-order livestock supply companies. In general, it is recommended to keep on hand:

❋ A broad-spectrum antibiotic such as Pen-G or LA-200

❋ Terramycin eye ointment and powder for poultry water

Alternative: Natural antibiotics include herbs, herbal tinctures, essential oils, homeopathic remedies, etc. Which to get will depend on your health philosophy. See Finding an Alternative Medicine Veterinarian and Books for Your Homestead Library under Resources.

Medications for Digestive Problems

Medications for digestive problems are given orally. Liquids are easiest to administer with a dosing syringe. Pastes come in tubes with a dial to set the dosage according to the animal's weight. Powders can be mixed with water and given by mouth with a syringe. Options include:

❋ Baking soda to prevent bloat

❋ Mineral oil to treat bloat

❋ Kao-Pec, Pepto-Bismol, or Maalox to treat scours (must also treat the cause!)

❋ Activated charcoal if poisoning is suspected

Nutritional Support and Other Treatments

Nutritional supplements such as the following are given orally except where injections are indicated.

* Apple cider vinegar (preferably raw, organic) for potassium and to acidify urine; added to drinking water.

* B complex (injectable) for treating lethargy and appetite loss.

* Electrolytes or Pedialyte, powdered or liquid, for dehydration.

* Ferrodex, injectable iron for anemic animals.

* Probiotic powder or paste, or live culture yogurt or kefir. Probiotics are important for healthy digestion. These are especially important if you are also giving antibiotics. For powder or paste follow instructions on the label. For yogurt or kefir, administer with a dosing syringe.

* Prevent urinary calculi by adding ammonium chloride to drinking water.

* Tetanus antitoxin is an injectable given to a wounded animal to prevent tetanus. It's also often given before castrating males.

HOW TO KNOW WHEN YOU NEED A VET

You suspect something might be wrong, but how can you be sure? How do you know when you need the vet? The following are clues that something might be wrong.

Change in Behavior

If you've been spending regular time observing your animals then any of the following changes in behavior may indicate a health problem.

If you observe more than one, the next step would be to take your animal's vital signs for more information.

- Isolation
- Not eating
- Ruminants stop chewing cud
- Teeth grinding
- Head down
- Listless, disinterested in surroundings
- Stumbling or circling
- Lying down more than usual
- Weak

Other Observable Symptoms

Any of the following may indicate something is wrong:

- Shivering or shaking
- Unusual posture or gait, such as limping or lameness
- Discharge from eyes, nose, or mouth
- Blisters on mouth, feet, or teats
- Hair loss or skin rashes
- Changes in manure
  - » Frequency
  - » Consistency: hard, soft, liquid
  - » Color
  - » Smell
- Changes in urination
  - » Appears difficult or painful
  - » Change in the amount
  - » Change in color
- Gums and inner eyelids should be bright pink. Paleness points to anemia. Causes could be internal parasites (do a fecal exam for a parasite egg count) or nutritional deficiencies (if the fecal count is low, a blood test may be helpful)
- Udder problems
  - » Tender to touch
  - » Harder than usual
  - » Hot or very warm to touch (mastitis)
- Pea-like lump blocking milk flow in teats
- Blistered teats
- Presence of blood in milk
- Clotted milk

VITAL SIGNS

Any time you think something might be off, check vital signs before contacting your vet or mentor. Sources vary on normal ranges, but typically you can expect the following in healthy animals. Temperatures are taken rectally. Count heart rate with a stethoscope.

NORMAL RANGE OF VITAL SIGNS

	TEMPERATURE	HEART RATE (BEATS PER MINUTE)	RESPIRATION (BREATHS PER MINUTE)	RUMEN MOVEMENTS (PER MINUTE)
CATTLE	101 to 102.8°F (38.3 to 38.9°C)	40 to 70	10 to 30	1 to 2
GOATS	101.5 to 103.5°F (38.6 to 39.7°C)	70 to 80	Adults 10 to 30; kids 20 to 40	1 to 2
PIGS	101.6 to 103.6°F (38.6 to 39.7°C)	60 to 100	8 to 18	N/A
POULTRY	105 to 109.4°F (40.5 to 43°C)	250 to 300	12 to 36	N/A
RABBITS	101.3 to 104°F (38.5 to 40.0°C)	130 to 325	30 to 60	N/A
SHEEP	100.9 to 103.8°F (38.3 to 39.8°C)	60 to 90	12 to 20	1 to 2

DIAGNOSIS AND TREATMENT

Figuring out what's wrong is difficult with animals. Your critters can't tell you when something hurts or that they don't feel well. You will have to rely on observation, a physical examination, and vital signs. Always isolate the animal. This will limit the others' exposure plus protect the sick animal from being picked on or bullied.

When should you call your vet? Any time you are uncertain about what's going on. If you don't have someone available, there are several internet groups that can be helpful in emergencies. See Online Forums Where You Can Ask Questions in Resources.

WHEN DEATH IS KINDER THAN PROLONGING LIFE

We once had a Nubian goat that broke her shoulder. The vet recommended we put her down. We weren't emotionally ready for that and tried to treat her at home. Eventually she gave up. Our choices were to either let her starve to death in depression and pain, or put her down as quickly and humanely as possible. We decided to take her to a meat processor, because that gave her purpose, even in death. That may seem strange in an age when it's common to spend thousands of dollars on veterinary medications and treatments, usually for beloved pets. For livestock, this usually isn't practical, especially if the animal cannot regain functional health. Even for those with a no-kill philosophy, there eventually comes a time when it is cruel to allow an animal to suffer. For example, advanced disease, severe maiming by a predator, or being hit by a vehicle.

Humane Killing

There are several options:

❋ Have your veterinarian do it

❋ Hire someone to do it

❋ Do it yourself

Veterinarians can give lethal injections, but that option is not available to the public. The next most humane option is shooting for large livestock, or a sharp knife for poultry and rabbits. The procedure is the same as for slaughtering for meat, so see that section in Chapter 7. If the animal is not diseased, it can be butchered for meat or pet food. Also, you will need a proper disposal plan for the carcass. Acceptable disposal may include burying, incinerating, composting, and rendering (commercial recycling of animal carcasses and waste). Most states have laws regulating these, so check with your state agricultural office before proceeding.

CHAPTER 9

KEEPING THEM SAFE

One of the hard realities of keeping livestock is loss from predation. Sometimes you will find remains, or sometimes animals will completely disappear. Predation may be a recurring problem or it may be seasonal, for example, during hawk migration or when coyotes are feeding pups.

When you have missing animals or find remains, you want to know what caused it. This chapter will give you an idea of what predators are common, what they prey on, and how to identify them by what they leave behind. A good book on identifying animal tracks may also be helpful. I'll give you information on predator control and deterrents, plus other ways to protect your livestock.

COMMON LIVESTOCK PREDATORS

ANIMAL	PREYS ON	SIGNS OF ATTACK
BADGERS	Poultry Rabbits Young kids Lambs	Consume everything except the head and fur along the back May bury parts of larger kill in holes resembling dens
BEARS	All livestock and pets	Kill by biting the neck or slapping the head Carcass torn, mauled, and mutilated May eat udders of females Gut opened, heart and liver consumed, intestines spread out around the kill site Carcass may be partially skinned Feces often found in the kill area
BOBCATS AND LYNX	Sheep Goats Poultry Rabbits Domestic cats	Kill larger prey by attacking and tearing trachea Kill smaller prey and poultry by biting head or neck Claw marks on both sides of carcass Prefer to consume hindquarters, shoulder, and neck Often cover the remains with litter
DOMESTIC CATS	Young poultry and rabbits	Messy attack site leaving fur and feathers Consume meaty portions of carcass Exposed bones gnawed
COYOTES	Goats Kids Sheep Lambs Calves Pigs Rabbits Poultry Small pets	Attack at night, dawn, or dusk Bolder in isolated areas May dig under fences or chew through poultry netting Usually kill by biting the throat May leave puncture wounds on head, neck, or front shoulders Rumen and intestines may be dragged away from the carcass May dismember carcass to eat Chew calf tails Tend to leave scat on elevated surfaces such as a log or rock

COMMON LIVESTOCK PREDATORS

ANIMAL	PREYS ON	SIGNS OF ATTACK
DOMESTIC DOGS	Goats Sheep Calves Pigs Rabbits Domestic cats Poultry	Attack hindquarters, flanks, but also neck and front shoulders Often tear victim's ears Severely mutilate but rarely eat the kill Multiple kills common Often seen in the vicinity prior to the kill May eat eggs
EAGLES	Poultry Young goats Young sheep	Distinctive puncture marks from talons Leave skeleton intact with head and neck attached Frequently feed on the brain along with meat from other portions of the carcass
FISHERS/ FISHER CATS	Poultry Rabbits Domestic pets	Good climbers and diggers Typically hunt at night Attack from behind Will raid chicken coops for eggs Multiple kills
FOXES	Poultry Rabbits Piglets Domestic cats Young lambs Kids	May dig under fences or chew through chicken wire Catch by the throat and kill by biting neck and back Prey will have broken necks Single birds are usually carried off leaving only feathers and a small amount of blood In a coop, foxes can get into a killing frenzy and kill the entire flock Breasts and legs of birds eaten first Other body parts scattered or partially buried Break open eggs and lick contents clean from shell
HAWKS	Poultry Rabbits Domestic pets Young lambs Kids	Attack from above Hunt during the day, especially near dusk and dawn Kill one at a time Head eaten Pluck prey, leaving piles of feathers on the ground

COMMON LIVESTOCK PREDATORS

ANIMAL	PREYS ON	SIGNS OF ATTACK
HOGS (FERAL)	Kids Lambs Small goats Small sheep	Typically eat entire carcass May carry off carcass Tracks and blood at feeding site may be only evidence
MINK	Poultry	Good climbers Kill by biting through head, upper neck, or jugular vein Multiple small bites on body Multiple birds killed Often eat only heads of victims Bodies may be neatly piled Eat eggs by breaking the ends
MOUNTAIN LIONS (ALSO CALLED COUGARS, PUMAS, AND PANTHERS)	Cattle Sheep Goats Pigs	Multiple animals killed Kill by biting top of skull, neck, or spinal column Eat front quarters and neck of prey first Stomach typically untouched Victim may have multiple broken bones Carcass often dragged off, covered with litter, and fed on for several days Carcass often moved for each feeding
OPOSSUMS	Poultry	Night attacks Will kill and eat adult birds near the coop Chicks and eggs often carried off Birds mauled Abdomen eaten Messy when eating eggs Usually kill only one at a time
OWLS	Poultry Rabbits Domestic pets	Night attacks, usually on birds roosting outdoors at night Bloody puncture marks in back and breast Often remove and eat the head and neck of their prey Carry off victim, so no trace

COMMON LIVESTOCK PREDATORS

ANIMAL	PREYS ON	SIGNS OF ATTACK
RACCOONS	Poultry	Can often figure out how to open door latches
		Go for head and neck
		Crop and breast torn and chewed
		Entrails eaten
		May pull head or leg through the cage and leave body behind
		You may find the head a distance away
		Multiple birds killed in one attack
		Eggs may be removed from nest and eaten nearby
RATS	Poultry babies Eggs	Disappearing chicks and eggs
		Partially eaten bodies
		Carcasses often dragged into holes or concealed places
SKUNKS	Poultry Eggs Beehives	Usually nocturnal
		Good diggers
		Usually kill chicks
		May kill one or two adults during a visit
		Victim mauled considerably with multiple bites
		Abdomen eaten
		Unmistakable lingering smell
		Eggs are opened at one end as though the chick hatched
		Eggs may be removed from nest but usually not far
SNAKES	Poultry babies	Chicks and eggs disappear
		Snake skins lying about
		May hide in coop
WEASELS	Poultry	Kill by biting through head, upper neck, or jugular vein
		Multiple birds killed
		Often eat only heads of victims
		Multiple small bites on body
		Bodies neatly piled
		Eat eggs by breaking the ends

COMMON LIVESTOCK PREDATORS

ANIMAL	PREYS ON	SIGNS OF ATTACK
WOLVES	Cattle	Attack by cutting or damaging the muscles and ligaments in the back legs or flanks
		Slash-like teeth marks may be found on the rear legs and flanks
		Victims are usually disemboweled

PREDATOR CONTROL

Raccoons in a live animal trap

Before taking action, check federal and state laws and regulations regarding wild predators. Some are protected by wildlife law, others have legal hunting seasons. Check city and county laws regarding domestic dogs. Although rural areas don't usually have leash laws, there may be regulations regarding roaming dogs and how you are legally allowed to deal with dogs attacking your livestock.

Animal control. May or may not be able to help, but can advise you on a course of action.

Killing. This can be controversial, especially among people who don't understand the real-life problems of protecting livestock. In general, killing an animal is a temporary solution, because it won't eliminate the possibility of another of its species taking its place.

❋ Poisons: These have the potential to kill animals other than their targets, including pets and other livestock.

❋ Shooting: Know the law for this method of protecting your livestock. Small game (raccoon, opossum, snake) is edible.

❋ Trapping and drowning: Often used for rodents and small predators.

❋ Hunting: Know your state's hunting laws, including seasons and limits.

Live animal traps. This is usually considered more humane than killing, but there are a couple of considerations in regards to relocating predators and pests.

Don't let your solution become someone else's problem. Relocating a predator to where it can kill and maim someone else's pets or livestock is bad form. The golden rule applies here—would you want someone to relocate their problem predators close to you?

When you relocate an animal, you will be placing it in unfamiliar territory. It will not know where to find water, food, and protective shelter. Your kindness may not be as kind as you think.

PREDATOR DETERRENTS

Loss from predation is an unfortunate reality, but you can minimize it with these precautions.

Fencing. Fencing is your first line of defense. See the discussion on fencing in Chapter 3. Always keep fences in good repair and fence lines clear of brush to deter predators from spying on your stock.

* If you have a coyote problem, be aware that coyotes can jump about 5 to 5½ feet. Walk fence lines frequently to check for areas needing repair.

* If you have problems with digging predators (coyotes or foxes), run an electric hot wire on the outside of the fence close to the ground.

Guardian animals. Livestock dogs, llamas, or donkeys can be useful, especially for goats and sheep.

Not all breeds of dogs are suited to being *livestock guardian dogs* (LGDs). Dogs are predators themselves and have the instinct to hunt, especially when they form a pack. Common LGD breeds include Great Pyrenees, Anatolian Shepherd, Bernese Mountain Dog, Maremma, and Komondor.

LGDs are usually very expensive to buy, and there are no guarantees that any particular individual will make a good guardian. There is some training involved, but it helps if the dog has a natural aptitude for the task. Choose puppies from farms or homesteads where the parents are working dogs, actively guarding livestock.

Llamas and goats

Llamas often make good guardians, with some individuals being more natural at it than others. They are territorial and, without other llamas, tend to bond with their pasture mates. They are more economical to keep and feed than dogs, and require no guardian training. Their best use as guardians is against small predators such as foxes or single coyotes or dogs. They are no match for an aggressive pack of coyotes, dogs, or wolves, or against bears or mountain lions.

Donkeys are sometimes used as guardians, with some being more natural at it than others. They are territorial and tend to be aggressive toward pasture intruders, especially those of the canine family. They are no match for aggressive packs, bears, or mountain lions.

Other animal deterrents. Roosters are always on the alert and quick to sound an alarm. Crows dislike hawks and will actively chase them away.

Presence of human activity. Most predators are shy, so it is helpful to check on your livestock frequently, walk your fence lines often, and generally make your presence known.

Nighttime securement of stock. If you are able, put your critters indoors for the night. This is commonly done with poultry, but can also be done with other livestock, unless your herd and flock numbers exceed housing space.

Daytime securement of stock. Chicken tractors can be used for poultry. For all species, keep young in areas closest to the barn and house, where you can keep an eye on them.

Decoys and scarecrows. These are only effective if they are moved frequently.

Lights and noise. Motion detector lights at night or radios during the day can be useful. If you use lights, keep your stock from becoming visible by letting the lights shine out and away from the barn or barnyard pens.

CHAPTER 10

KEEPING THINGS MANAGEABLE

Homestead burnout: It's not something you think about when you first get started, but it does happen. Things start well but soon become overwhelming: too many projects, too little time, too many things going wrong. The workload gets heavier, the to-do list gets longer, and there are never-ending demands on your time and energy. Things aren't working out the way you expected and the dream has become a nightmare. Changing lifestyles is a huge undertaking. In this chapter I'll share the lessons Dan and I have learned about how to keep things manageable.

UNDERSTAND YOUR MOTIVATION

Enthusiasm makes a great start, but it takes commitment to stay the course. Your motive for homesteading is the foundation of your commitment. If I were to ask you why you want to homestead, how would you answer? Because everybody else is doing it? Because it sounds like fun? Because you like the country? Because you don't like your job or the life you live now? Or because you have a conviction that it's the best way to live in a world that seems to be falling apart? Your answer should help your prioritize your goals and stick to them.

To keep things manageable, you need a prime directive and the conviction to stick to it.

MAKE A PLAN

When we bought our property we had a long list of things we wanted to do, but no idea how to begin. To help us visualize and prioritize our ideas, Dan suggested that we make a map of our property. We started with existing features and drew in the things we wanted to add: gardens, orchard, greenhouse, and barn. We call this our "master plan," and have found it indispensable in discussing new ideas and setting goals.

I recommend that you do the same. Ask yourself how you would like to see your homestead in five years. Ten years? Twenty? Make a map of your property and draw it as you want it to be. That drawing is your long-term visual plan for your homestead.

To keep things manageable, you need to know what you want to accomplish.

SET GOALS AND PRIORITIZE

Once you have a primary goal and a plan for your homestead you can begin to organize and prioritize your steps to getting there. Evaluate your steps in terms of your primary goal, then prioritize your projects according to how well they enable you to reach that goal. Projects that help you fulfill your plan take priority.

To keep things manageable, make a list of secondary goals and prioritize them according to how well they help you toward your primary goal.

START SLOWLY, START SMALL

Excitement in the beginning makes it hard to be patient and easy to start on too many fronts at once. But too much too soon can rapidly become overwhelming, and unfortunately, things have a way of not going as planned. I can't tell you how often a simple repair turns into a major rebuild. Or an unexpected windstorm drops an old tree onto the fence. Or an animal gets sick or hurt.

To keep things manageable, choose to work on only one or two of your most important goals until they are accomplished, and expect the unexpected.

REVIEW AND REVISE

Once a year, sit down with your plan and your list of goals. Review what you've accomplished and what is yet to be done. Ask yourself, what's working? What isn't? It's likely that in the course of the year you have figured out that some things are heavy on time and energy, but light on benefit. Or maybe you found a workaround to some of your goals. Maybe your priorities have changed. Maybe circumstances have changed. Or maybe after experimenting with a few things for a while, you've changed your thinking and want to change your plan altogether.

To keep things manageable, take time to evaluate, be flexible, and adapt your plan and goals as needed.

DAY-TO-DAY MANAGEMENT

Keep a To-Do List

When there's a lot to be done, a to-do list is invaluable. It keeps you from getting distracted and feeling scattered. It's rewarding to cross things off. Plus, it's easier to prioritize a written list than a mental one. Date each list, prioritize it, and work on one item at a time. Whatever doesn't get done one day is put on the next day's list.

To keep things manageable, keep a checklist and refer to it often.

Routine Is Your Friend

When you have a routine, the day seems to flow. There is no deliberating what to do next, you just do it. Things rarely get forgotten, because you take care of necessities by habit. Even your projects have a time niche.

Animals respond very well to predictability, and how you determine your routine is up to you. There is nothing that says you have to do the milking at 5 a.m. and 5 p.m. If you want to milk at 10 and 10, that's up to you! Choose times that work best with your schedule. If a routine must be changed, expect confusion for a while. Things will settle down again once your critters learn the new routine.

To keep things manageable, develop a routine and stick with it.

Give Yourself Permission to Make Mistakes

Most of us are learning as we go. You will make mistakes, and even when you're doing your best, bad things will happen. It's especially difficult when the bad things involve injury, disease, or death to an animal. The attitude you take is important. You can let discouragement convince you that all your problems and mistakes are failures. Or you can view them as unfortunate lessons that have gifted you with information that can pave the way for long-term success. I can honestly say that I've learned more from problems and mistakes than I have from getting things right the first time.

To keep things manageable, accept that mistakes are a part of life.

THE LONG RUN

Everything Takes Longer Than Planned

Dan and I used to put time frames on our projects: installing a new energy-efficient window should take half a day, and we should have that new wall done by June. Unfortunately, it never works out that way! Gradually we've learned to take it one day at a time and say, "When it's done, it's done!"

To keep things manageable, keep your schedule flexible and mentally allow for setbacks and delays.

You Can't Do It All

For every to-do list that I make, there are always things that don't get done. Usually these are placed on the next list, then the next list, and sometimes the list after that. It took me a while to accept that I can't do it all and to stop scolding myself for it. I may not get around to making a keyhole herb garden this year, but there's always another year.

To keep things manageable, be willing to set things aside if you need to.

Keep a Day of Rest

Most of the advice I've read about avoiding homestead burnout recommends taking an annual vacation. The problem is that for most homesteaders a real vacation isn't practical. Even if we can manage to find someone knowledgeable and willing enough to care for our livestock for a week or two, it usually isn't financially feasible.

Instead of taking vacations, Dan and I keep a day of rest. One day every week is set aside to rest, relax, and reset our minds, bodies, and spirits. On that day we set aside projects and nonessential activities.

The animals must be tended, but building, planting, housework, repair jobs, etc., are set aside for the day.

For us, this 7-day cycle works better than a vacation. We don't get a 7-day break once a year, we get 52 24-hour breaks throughout the year.

To keep things manageable, set aside a day for a weekly break and do something you enjoy.

Learn to Think Seasonally

There are several aspects to seasonal thinking. Seasonal eating is one, but the work on a homestead is seasonal too. In the beginning there is so much to do that we tend to prioritize according to greatest need. As things takes shape, much of what you need to do is by season: planting, harvesting, food preservation, and wood chopping, for example. Plan your year by starting with these seasonal activities, then schedule your other projects around them. Your break comes in winter, when there is less to do and more time to pursue other things you enjoy.

To keep things manageable, learn to live by the ebb and flow of the seasons.

Consider a Visitor Policy

One day you get an email from family or friends announcing they are coming for a visit! They want to get away from it all, see your farm, play with the animals, eat big country breakfasts, take tractor rides, hike in the woods, and spend leisurely afternoons on the front porch swing sipping iced tea. Oh, and they invited cousin Jake's kids, because his wife really needs a break and they knew you wouldn't mind, so there will be 12 of them. They'll only stay for a week or two, and what a great place for summer vacations!

Hopefully your family and friends are willing to pitch in when they come for a visit, but sometimes, folks don't understand that just because you aren't "at work" you are still working. One pitfall of visitors is finding yourself playing the cordial host every time you have company, especially when you have more to do than time to do it. If you can't take the time off, say so, or invite them to give you a hand and assure them you really could use the help. Make extended visits "work parties," and use the extra hands to get big projects done. Assign daily chores as part of that authentic farm experience. If your visitors are local, use your day of rest for visiting.

To keep things manageable, lay ground rules for visitors up front if you need to.

Preparedness with Livestock Is a Lifestyle

Most kinds of preparedness can be achieved with a checklist. Many prepper lists are available to help you prepare for both short-term emergencies and long-term crises. Prepping with livestock, however, is a lifestyle. Their well-being requires a relationship—a partnership—with you. Your side of the partnership is to provide food, water, shelter, safety, health care, and whatever it takes to keep them happy and productive. They provide food, manure, brush control, companionship, and endless entertainment. Both partners benefit.

To keep things manageable, don't just think of yourself as a prepper, but as a partner with your animals and your land.

CONCLUSION: IF SHTF

So, what happens if SHTF? What if we were struck by an electromagnetic pulse, coronal mass ejection, nuclear holocaust, or economic collapse? It's not something we hope will happen, but it's a question that's often on my mind, because Dan and I are still in transition too.

If SHTF, I would have to make some hard decisions. I would have to know how many animals our land can support and adjust their numbers accordingly.

If SHTF, I wouldn't have access to information stored or bookmarked on my computer. To prepare for this, I have a hard copy notebook for printouts and handwritten notes on information I may need.

If SHTF, I would need to know how to use the manual tools and alternative technology we have invested in. Dan and I use electric- or gasoline-powered tools and equipment for their time savings, but for each of these we have low-tech alternatives and have learned how to use them.

If SHTF, I would have security concerns for our homestead and especially our livestock. The likelihood of civil chaos on an extensive scale means having a defense strategy in place is prudent.

My encouragement to you is to make a start in preparedness if you haven't already done so. Hope for the best, plan for the worst, and take it one step at a time. At the very least, your life will be all the richer for learning to partner with livestock.

BIBLIOGRAPHY

"All About Chicken Predators." Accessed December 3, 2017. http://professorchickenspredators.webs.com.

Arczewska-Włosek, Anna and Sylwester Świątkiewicz. "Herbs as an Effective Tool in Coccidiosis Control," *INTERMAG*. Accessed November 29, 2017. http://farmhealth.eu/news/herbs-as-an-effective-tool-in-coccidiosis-control.

Ashbrook, Frank G. *Butchering, Processing and Preservation of Meat.* New York: Van Nostrand Reinhold Co., 1955.

Asher, David. *The Art of Natural Cheesemaking.* White River Junction, VT: Chelsea Green Publishing, 2015.

"Beeswax Recipes," *Beeswax from Beekeepers.* Accessed January 7, 2018. https://beeswaxfrombeekeepers.com/beeswaxrecipes.

"Breed Standards," *American Goat Society.* Accessed August 7, 2017. http://americangoatsociety.com/education/breed_standards.php.

"Breed Standards," *Miniature Dairy Goat Society.* Accessed August 9, 2017. http://miniaturedairygoats.net/breed-standards_page.html.

Carter, Kevin. "The Christmas Pie," *Savoring the Past,* modified December 19, 2012. Accessed January 11, 2018. https://savoringthepast.net/2012/12/19/the-christmas-pie.

Coffey, Linda. "Coccidiosis: Symptoms, Prevention, and Treatment in Sheep, Goats, and Calves," *ATTRA Sustainable Agriculture,* modified April 12, 2016. Accessed November 20, 2017. https://attra.ncat.org/attra-pub/viewhtml.php?id=483.

"Commercial Feed Alternatives," *Frog Chorus Farm*. Accessed December 31, 2017. http://www.frogchorusfarm.com/FeedingRabbits.html.

"Control of Lice and Mange Mites in Cattle," *Organic Agriculture Centre of Canada*. Accessed December 1, 2017. https://cdn.dal.ca/content/dam/dalhousie/pdf/faculty/agriculture/oacc/en/livestock/Welfare/Lice_control.pdf.

Damerow, Gail. *Fence for Pasture & Garden*. Pownal, VT: Storey Communications, Inc., 1992.

Decker, Fred. "How to Cure a Country Ham at Home," *Leaf*. Accessed January 10, 2018. https://www.leaf.tv/articles/how-to-cure-a-country-ham-at-home.

Dohner, Jan. "Guardian Llamas: Pros and Cons," *Mother Earth News*. Accessed December 5, 2017. https://www.motherearthnews.com/homesteading-and-livestock/guardian-llamas-zbcz1309.

Dohner, Jan. "Using a Donkey as a Livestock Guardian: The Pros and Cons," *Mother Earth News*. Accessed December 5, 2017. https://www.motherearthnews.com/homesteading-and-livestock/guard-donkey-zbcz1310.

"Egg Incubation Periods." Accessed October 28, 2017. http://asby.com.sg/period.htm.

Emery, Carla. *The Encyclopedia of Country Living*. Seattle, WA: Sasquatch Books, 1994.

Evangelista, Anita. *How to Live Without Electricity—And Like It*. Port Townsend, WA: Breakout Productions, 1997.

"Farm Water Supply Requirements," *Alberta Agriculture and Forestry*. Accessed January 1, 2018. https://www1.agric.gov.ab.ca/$department/deptdocs.nsf/all/agdex1349.

Gardeners & Farmers of Centre Terre Vivante. *Preserving Food without Freezing or Canning.* White River Junction, VT: Chelsea Green Publishing, 2007.

"Heritage Turkey," *The Livestock Conservancy.* Accessed September 5, 2017. http://livestockconservancy.org/index.php/resources/internal/heritage-turkey.

"Is Tethering of Farm Animals Acceptable? " *RSPCA Australia Knowledgebase.* Accessed October 8, 2017. http://kb.rspca.org.au/Is-tethering-of-farm-animals-acceptable_400.html.

Kennard, Dwight C., et al. *Research bulletin. 843: The Use of Compost (Built-up) Litter in Chicken Houses.* Wooster, OH: Ohio Agricultural Experiment Station, 1959.

Kirberger, Roberta. "More About Milk Sheep: Ewes, Lambing and Feeding Tips," *Mother Earth News,* July/August 1975. Accessed November 7, 2017. https://www.motherearthnews.com/homesteading-and-livestock/more-about-milk-sheep-zm0z75zkon.

LaShell, Beth. "Mineral Deficiencies," *Fort Lewis College,* April 11, 2005. Accessed November 10, 2017. http://faculty.fortlewis.edu/LASHELL_B/mineral deficiencies.pdf

LaShell, Beth, "Vitamin Deficiencies," *Fort Lewis College*, March 30, 2005. Accessed November 10, 2017. faculty.fortlewis.edu/LASHELL_B/vitamin deficiencies.pdf.

Lawrence, Shannon. "Urinary Calculi in Goats," *Hoegger Supply Company.* Accessed December 5, 2017. http://hoeggerfarmyard.com/urinary-calculi-in-goats.

"Livestock and Animal Predation Identification," *Internet Center for Wildlife Damage Management,* 2015. Accessed November 24, 2017. http://icwdm.org/Inspection/Livestock.aspx.

Martok. "Vital Signs—Part 1," *Hobby Farms*. Accessed November 14, 2017. www.hobbyfarms.com/vital-signs-part-1.

Moechnig, Howard. "Improving and Sustaining Forage Production in Pastures," *Minnesota Department of Agriculture*, 2010. Accessed December 10, 2017. www.mda.state.mn.us/~/media/Files/animals/grazingimprove.ashx.

NCAT Staff. "Predator Control for Sustainable & Organic Livestock Production," *ATTRA Sustainable Agriculture*. Accessed November 22, 2017. https://attra.ncat.org/attra-pub/summaries/summary.php?pub=189.

Nelson, Mark Loge. "Feed-ology: How to Read a Feed Tag," *Washington State University,* July 2014. Accessed January 5, 2018. http://cru.cahe.wsu.edu/CEPublications/FS138E/FS138E.pdf.

O'Connor, Michael. "Heat Detection and Timing of Insemination for Cattle," *PennState Extension,* 1993, https://extension.psu.edu/heat-detection-and-timing-of-insemination-for-cattle.

Pesaturo, Janet. "Poultry Predator Identification: A Guide to Tracks and Sign," *One Acre Farm*. Accessed November 30, 2017. http://ouroneacrefarm.com/poultry-predator-identification-a-guide-to-tracks-and-sign.

Plamondon, Robert. "FAQ: Deep Litter in Chicken Coops," *Practical Poultry Tips*. Accessed September 16, 2017. http://www.plamondon.com/wp/deep-litter-chicken-coops.

Pritchard, Forrest. "How to Raise Pigs on Pasture," *On Pasture*, modified April 21, 2014. Accessed September 31, 2017. http://onpasture.com/2014/04/21/how-to-raise-pigs-on-pasture.

"Processing Ducks and Geese," *Metzer Farms*. Accessed January 9, 2018. http://www.metzerfarms.com/ProcessingWaterfowl.cfm.

Raines, Christopher, R. "The Butcher Kept Your Meat?" *Penn State University*. Accessed January 9, 2018. http://animalscience.psu.edu/extension/meat/pdf/The Butcher Stole My Meat.pdf.

Ramsay, Irene. "Natural Ways of Treating Mastitis," *U-Say Ranch*, modified April 7, 2000. Accessed December 2, 2017. http://u-say ranch.com/2010/01/natural-ways-of-treating-mastitis-by-irene-ramsay.

Reith, Sue. "Hypocalcemia—Ca and Ph in the Diet," *Dairy Goat Care and Management*. Accessed November 20, 2017. http://goats.wikifoundry.com/page/Hypocalcemia + - + Ca + and + Ph + in + the + diet.

Ruhlman, Michael, and Polcyn, Brian. *Charcuterie: The Craft of Salting, Smoking, and Curing*. New York: W. W. Norton & Company, 2005.

Rush, Ivan G., and Groteleuschen, Dale. "G79-465 Urinary Calculi (Waterbelly) in Cattle and Sheep," *University of Nebraska*, modified April 1996. Accessed December 5, 2017. https://digitalcommons .unl.edu/extensionhist/333.

Schivera, Diane. "Raising Organic Pigs," *Maine Organic Farmers and Gardeners Association*. Accessed September, 30, 2017. http://www.mofga.org/Portals/2/Fact Sheets/FS 16 Organic Pigs.pdf.

Schivera, Diane. "Raising Rabbits on Pasture," *Maine Organic Farmers and Gardeners Association*. Accessed January 1, 2018. http://www.mofga.org/Publications/MaineOrganicFarmerGardener/Winter20092010/Rabbits/tabid/1392.

"Skylines Internal Parasite Control Program," *Skylines Farm*. Accessed December 10, 2017. http://skylinesfarm.com/parasite control.htm.

Stanley, Jennifer. "Preparing Salt Pork," *Savoring the Past.* Accessed January 11, 2018. https://savoringthepast.net/2016/03/30/preparing-salt-pork.

Tate, Leigh. *How to Bake Without Baking Powder.* NP: Kikobian Books, 2016.

Tate, Leigh. *How to Garden for Goats.* NP: Kikobian Books, 2015.

Tate, Leigh. *How to Get Cream from Goats' Milk.* NP: Kikobian Books, 2016.

Tate, Leigh. *How to Mix Feed Rations with the Pearson Square.* NP: Kikobian Books, 2015.

Tate, Leigh. *How to Preserve Eggs.* NP: Kikobian Bosoks, 2014.

Terry, Scott M. "The Handy Homestead Reference Sheets," *North Country Farmer*, 2017. http://northcountryfarmer.com/?p=1587

Terry, Scott M. "How to Prevent and Naturally Treat Mastitis in the Family Milk Cow," *North Country Farmer.* Accessed December 3, 2017. http://northcountryfarmer.com/?p=320.

Thomas Paine Ditto Works. "How to Raise Milk Sheep: From Lambing to Sheep Milk Production," *Mother Earth News*, September/October 1974. Accessed November 7, 2017. https://www.motherearthnews.com/homesteading-and-livestock/milk-sheep-zm0z74zkon.

Ussery, Harvey and Ellen. "The Homestead Waterfowl Flock," *The Modern Homestead.* Accessed September 5, 2017. http://www.themodernhomestead.us/article/Waterfowl-1.html.

Ussery, Harvey and Ellen. "When Life Gives You Lemons," *TheModern Homestead.* Accessed September 19, 2017. http://www.themodernhomestead.us/article/Deep-Litter-1.html.

Victorian Farmers Federation. "Livestock Factsheet: Mineral Deficiencies in Livestock." Accessed November 25, 2017. http://www.vff.org.au/vff/Documents/Factsheet_Livestock_Traceminerals.pdf.

Weaver, Sue. *The Backyard Cow: An Introductory Guide.* Pownal, VT: Storey Publishing, 2012.

Wells, Ann. "Integrated Parasite Management for Organic Dairy Cattle," *NODPA News*, May 2005. Accessed December 30, 2017. http://www.nodpa.com/ParasiteManagement/Integrated_Parasite_Management_May_2005.pdf.

"Worming with Food Grade Diatomaceous Earth," *Wolf Creek Ranch.* Accessed November 19, 2017. http://wolfcreekranchorganics.com/library/diatomaceous_earth_worming.html.

RESOURCES

Chapter 1:
First Things First

County Cooperative Extension Service Office

County Extension Office Map—www.pickyourown.org/county extensionagentoffices.htm

Find a Livestock Veterinarian

Local Ranch Vets—www.localranchvets.com

American Association of Small Ruminant Practitioners—www.aasrp.org

Also see Finding an Alternative Medicine Veterinarian under Chapter 8 Resources.

Livestock Laws and Ordinances

Chicken Laws and Ordinances (and How to Change Them)—www.backyardchickens.com/articles/chicken-laws-and-ordinances-and-how-to-change-them.65675

Urban Livestock Laws—www.urbanaglaw.org/animals-and-livestock

How to Change Urban Chicken Laws—www.communitychickens.com/backyard-poultry-and-chicken-laws-how-to-change-urban-chicken-laws

Urban Agriculture State Legislation—www.ncsl.org/research/agriculture-and-rural-development/urban-agriculture-state-legislation.aspx

How to Change a Law Through the Democratic Process—www.wikihow.com/Change-a-Law-Through-the-Democratic-Process

Chapter 2:
Best Breeds for Self-Reliance

The Livestock Conservancy—livestockconservancy.org

Cattle

Breeds—homesteadontherange.com/cattle-breeds

Dairy cows—www.wellfedhomestead.com/choosing-a-dairy-cow-breeds

Cattle Breed Comparison Chart—livestockconservancy.org/index.php/heritage/internal/cattle-chart

Goats

Goat Breed Comparison Chart—livestockconservancy.org/index.php/heritage/internal/goat-chart

Kinne's Minis—kinne.net/articles.htm

Onion Creek Ranch—www.tennesseemeatgoats.com/articles2/articlesMain.html

Fias Co Farm—https://fiascofarm.com

Sheep

Sheep 201: A Beginners Guide to Raising Sheep—www.sheep101.info/201/index.html

Sheep Breed Comparison Chart—livestockconservancy.org/index.php/heritage/internal/sheep-chart

Milking Sheep—www.milkingsheep.com

Pigs

Pig Breed Comparison Chart—livestockconservancy.org/index.php/heritage/internal/pig-chart

Pigs for Small Farms—journeytoforever.org/farm_pig.html

The Basics of Raising Pigs—www.mofga.org/Publications/Maine
OrganicFarmerGardener/Fall2007/Pigs/tabid/805/Default.aspx

Poultry

Henderson's Handy Dandy Chicken Chart—www.sagehenfarmlodi
.com/chooks/chooks.html

Poultry Breeds—livestockconservancy.org/index.php/heritage/
internal/poultry-breeds

Poultry for Small Farms—journeytoforever.org/farm_poultry.html

Guinea Fowl International—http://guineas.com

Rabbits

Rabbit Breed Comparison Chart—livestockconservancy.org/index
.php/heritage/internal/rabbit-chart

The Nature Trail: A Virtual Treasure Chest of Rabbit Information—
www.thenaturetrail.com

Online Forums Where You Can Ask Questions

Backyard Herds (all backyard livestock)—www.backyardherds.com

Keeping a Family Cow (cattle)—familycow.proboards.com

Dairy Goat Info (goats)—www.dairygoatinfo.com

The Lamb Pen (sheep)—www.thelambpen.com/forum

Pig Forum (pigs)—www.pigforum.com/forums

BackYard Chickens (poultry)—www.backyardchickens.com/forums

Rabbit Talk (rabbits)—http://rabbittalk.com

Chapter 3:
Barns, Shelters, and Fencing

Barn and Shelter Plans

How to Build Animal Housing: 60 Plans for Coops, Hutches, Barns, Sheds, Pens, Nestboxes, Feeders, Stanchions, and Much More, Carol Ekarius, Storey Publishing, 2004

North Dakota State University: Building Plans—www.ag.ndsu.edu/extension-aben/buildingplans

LSU AgCenter: Building Plans—www.lsuagcenter.com/portals/our_offices/departments/biological-ag-engineering/extension/building_plans

Milk Stand Plans

For goats

fiascofarm.com/goats/milkstand.html

www.sweetdeseret.com/wblog/?p=213

For cows

wagsranch.wordpress.com/2008/08/26/cow-milk-stanchion

zephyrhillfarm.blogspot.com/2013/07/our-dexter-milking-stanchion-plans.html

Solar Barn Lighting

Micro Solar—http://www.microsolarinc.com

Water

Water Storage: Tanks, Cisterns, Aquifers, and Ponds, Art Ludwig, Oasis Designs, 2011

Rainwater Catchment (At Last)—www.5acresandadream.com/2013/01/rainwater-catchment-at-last.html

Passive Solar Stock Tank—www.builditsolar.com/Projects/
WaterHeating/SolarHorseTank/SolarHorseTank.htm

Earth-heated Waterers by Cobett—cobett.com

Remote Winter Watering Systems—www.extension.umn.edu/
agriculture/beef/components/pdfs/Winter_watering_systems.pdf

Chapter 4:
Forage and Feed

Soil Resources

Hands-On Agronomy: Understanding Soil Fertility & Fertilizer Use, Neal
Kinsey and Charles Waters, Acres U.S.A., 2009

National Geochemical Survey, soil minerals by county—https://
mrdata.usgs.gov/geochem/doc/averages/countydata.htm

Soil Testing

Kinsey Ag—kinseyag.com

Logan Labs—www.loganlabs.com/index.html

Soil Amendments

Seven Springs Farm—www.7springsfarm.com

Fertrell Soil Amendments

   www.fertrell.com/soilamendments.htm

   www.fertrell.com/othersoilamendments.htm

Pasture Management

Salad Bar Beef, Joel Salatin, Polyface, Inc., 1995

*Holistic Management: A Commonsense Revolution to Restore Our
Environment*, Allan Savory, Island Press, 2016

*Multi-Species Rotational Grazing to Maximize Food and Income in
a TEOTWAWKI World*—https://survivalblog.com/multi-species-

rotational-grazing-to-maximize-food-and-income-in-a-teotwawki-world-by-j-b

Recommended grazing heights of pasture plants—www2.ca.uky.edu/grazer/April12_Grazing_Heights.php

Forages and Pasture Management—https://extension.tennessee.edu/Rhea/Documents/Ag%20Documents/Small%20Ruminant%20Conference/Advanced%20Forage%20Production.pdf

Raising Meat Rabbits on Pasture: Intensive Grazing with Bunnies—https://www.motherearthnews.com/homesteading-and-livestock/rabbits-on-pasture-intensive-grazing-with-bunnies-zbcz1504

Hay Harvesting
European (Austrian) Scythes

Adjustable snaths: onescytherevolution.com/index.html

Custom-fitted snaths: scythesupply.com

Feed
Homegrown Whole Grains, Sara Pitzer, Storey Publishing, 2009

Alternative Feeds for Ruminants, North Dakota State University—www.ag.ndsu.edu/publications/livestock/alternative-feeds-for-ruminants

Build Your Own Hammer Mill—www.makeyourownpellets.com/hammermillplans.html

Pearson Square
How to Mix Feed Rations with the Pearson Square, Leigh Tate, Kikobian Books, 2015

Calculating protein with the Pearson Square—www.5acresandadream.com/2012/02/calculating-protein-with-pearson-square.html

Pearson Square Online Calculators

www.prechel.net/formula/pearson.htm

homesteadapps.com/app/free/feedcalc/pearsonsquare.php

Nutrient Testing

Check with your county cooperative extension office to see if your state offers feed testing. Or, submit feed samples to a lab such as the following:

Servi-Tech, www.servitechlabs.com/Services/FeedTesting/tabid/67/Default.aspx

Intertek, www.intertek.com/food/testing/animal-feed-inspection

Midwest Labs, www.midwestlabs.com/industries-we-serve/animal-feed

Poisonous and Edible Garden and Forage Plants

Toxins that Affect the Ruminant—poisonousplants.ansci.cornell.edu/ruminantlist.html

Plants poisonous to livestock—poisonousplants.ansci.cornell.edu/anispecies.html

Guide to Poisonous Plants searchable database—csuvth.colostate.edu/poisonous_plants/Plants/Search

Safe and toxic food lists for rabbits:

Rise and Shine Rabbitry, https://riseandshinerabbitry.com/2012/02/26/safe-food-list-for-rabbits

Save a Fluff, www.saveafluff.co.uk/rabbit-info/safe-foods-for-rabbits

White Wing Rabbitry, whitewingrabbitry.weebly.com/safe--toxic-plants.html

Poisonous Plant Antidotes—www.goatworld.com/health/plants/antidotes.shtml

Hydroponic Fodder

Step by Step Tutorial on Growing Sprouted Fodder (video)—www.youtube.com/watch?v=RX4VoV7DeG8

DIY Sprouted Fodder for Livestock—www.motherearthnews.com/homesteading-and-livestock/sprouted-fodder

Silage

Silage Making for Small Scale Farmers—pdf.usaid.gov/pdf_docs/Pnadq897.pdf

Chapter 5:
Breeding and Pregnancy

Anti-Mating Goat and Sheep Apron

House of Bacchus Pet Supplies—www.houseofbacchuspetsupplies.com/anti-mating-aprons-s/118.htm

Pregnancy Testing

P-Test urine pregnancy detection kit—www.emlabgenetics.com/Pages/PTEST.aspx

DG29 Blood Pregnancy Test—genex.crinet.com/page3429/DG29BloodPregnancyTest

Bovipreg pregnancy detection kit using blood or milk—www.twilcanada.com/bovipreg.php

Preg-Tone, small ultrasound device—www.rencocorp.com/product/preg-tone

Online Gestation Calculators

Cattle—www.cattletoday.com/gestation.shtml

Goats—americangoatsociety.com/education/gestation_calculator.php

Sheep—www.raisingsheep.net/sheep-gestation-calculator-and-table.html

Pigs—cpsswine.com/farrowing-calculator

Rabbits—gestationcalculator.com/other/rabbit-pregnancy-calculator

Online Gestation Charts

Cattle—www.cattlegestationchart.com

Goats—www.oklahomashowgoats.com/Breeders/Gestation.htm

Sheep—dorpersheep.org/education

Pigs—www.triplebsires.com/gestiontable.html

Rabbits—madhatterrabbits.files.wordpress.com/2013/05/rabbit-breeding-schedule.jpg

Chapter 7:
Eggs, Milk, and Meat

Milk Stand Plans
See Chapter 3 Resources

How to Milk Videos

How to Milk a Cow by Hand—www.youtube.com/watch?v=g6u-hGnCYsI

How to Hand-milk a Goat—www.youtube.com/watch?v=SwBSl69OuWw

How to Hand-milk Sheep—www.youtube.com/watch?v=QhHVpl75-6o

Inexpensive Milking Machines

For cows, goats, or sheep:

   Dansha Farms, www.danshafarms.com

   Udderly EZ Milker, udderlyez.com

For goats:

   Henry Milker, www.henrymilker.com

DIY milking machine with hand vacuum pump—www.woodyglen.com/diymilker.html

DIY milking machine with Foodsaver vacuum pump—
themobilehomewoman.com/?p = 14492

Teat Sprays, Dips, and Washes

Commercial—Fight Bac spray, http://www.fightbac.com

Homemade:

Fias Co Farm, fiascofarm.com/goats/teatdip-udderwash.html

Henry Milker, blog.henrymilker.com/2012/05/how-to-make-
your-own-udder-cleaner.html

Land of Havilah Herbals, landofhavilahfarm.com/loh/natural-
raising/my-holistic-methods/my-goat-milking-milk-handling-
procedure

D.I.Y. Bullseye, www.diybullseye.com/homemade-udder-wash-
for-dairy-animals/2

Milk Testing

Cows—spiritedrose.wordpress.com/jersey-cattle/how-to-produce-
quality-milk/milk-testing

Goats

adga.org/steps-for-adga-dhir

americangoatsociety.com/milkpail/dhi_rules_procedures.php

Cream Separators

Slavic Beauty (manual or electric)—www.slavicbeauty.net/cream-
separators

Lehman's electric model—www.lehmans.com/product/electric-cream-
separator

Lehman's manual model—www.lehmans.com/product/hand-
operated-cream-separator

How to Build a Cream Separator—www.noahsnet.com/how-to-build-
a-cream-separator

Butter Churns

Lehman's small hand crank—www.lehmans.com/product/kilner-butter-churn

Lehman's large hand crank—www.lehmans.com/product/lehmans-dazey-butter-churn

French Butter Keepers

James Sloss Pottery—www.frenchbutterdish.com/index.php

Lehman's butter crock—www.lehmans.com/product/ancient-style-butter-crock

Cultured Milk (Yogurt and Kefir)

Easy Peasy Homemade Yogurt—www.5acresandadream.com/2009/11/easy-peasy-homemade-yogurt.html

Dom's About Kefir Grains and Kefir—http://users.sa.chariot.net.au/~dna/kefirpage.html

Sources for kefir grains:

Kefir Lady, www.kefirlady.com

Happy Herbalist, www.happyherbalist.com/kefir-live-grains-milk-kefir

Cheese

The Art of Natural Cheesemaking: Using Traditional, Non-Industrial Methods and Raw Ingredients to Make the World's Best Cheeses, David Asher, Chelsea Green Publishing, 2015

How to make calf or kid rennet—fankhauserblog.wordpress.com/2007/05/18/rennet-home-made-illustrated

Cheese press plans (make your own):

fiascofarm.com/dairy/cheesepress.html

www.motherearthnews.com/diy/make-a-diy-cheese-press-zbcz1401

www.littlegreencheese.com/2013/06/pressing-cheese-at-home
.html

Meat Processing

Basic Butchering of Livestock & Game, John J. Mettler, Storey
Publishing, 1986

Slaughtering and Butchering—www.backwoodshome.com/
slaughtering-and-butchering

The Humane Slaughter Association—www.hsa.org.uk

Learning How to Pluck a Duck—www.5acresandadream.com/2017/
02/learning-how-to-pluck-duck.html

Ask The Meatman articles, videos, and supplies—www.askthemeatman
.com

Meat Canning

*The Prepper's Canning Guide: Affordably Stockpile a Lifesaving Supply
of Nutritious, Delicious, Shelf-Stable Foods*, Daisy Luther, Ulysses
Press, 2017

Meat Curing and Smoking

Meat Curing Methods—www.meatsandsausages.com/sausage-
making/curing/methods

Charcuterie: The Craft of Salting, Smoking, and Curing, Michael
Ruhlman and Brian Polcyn, W. W. Norton & Co., 2005

Smoking Food: A Beginner's Guide, Chris Dubbs and Dave Heberle,
Skyhorse Publishing, 2008

Treating Pelts and Hides

Tan Your Hide!, Phyllis Hobson, Storey Publishing, 1977

Off-Grid Storage

The Joy of Keeping a Root Cellar: Canning, Freezing, Drying, Smoking, and Preserving the Harvest, Jennifer Megyesi, Skyhorse Publishing, 2010

Zeer pots—https://sustainabilitybox.com/making-pot-pot-refrigerator

How to Live Without Electricity—and Like It, Anita Evangelista, Breakout Productions, 1997

Prepper's Total Grid Failure Handbook: Alternative Power, Energy Storage, Low Voltage Appliances and Other Lifesaving Strategies for Self-Sufficient Living, Alan Fiebig and Arlene Fiebig, Ulysses Press, 2017

Chapter 8:
Keeping Them Healthy

Finding an Alternative Medicine Veterinarian

American Holistic Veterinary Medical Association—www.ahvma.org

Academy of Veterinary Homeopathy—theavh.org/referrals

American Veterinary Chiropractic Association—www.animalchiropractic.org

Veterinary Botanical Medicine Association—www.vbma.org/us-members.html

Books for Your Homestead Library

Complete Herbal Handbook for Farm and Stable, Juliette de Bairacli Levy, Faber & Faber, 1991

Alternative Treatments for Ruminant Animals, Paul Detloff, Acres U.S.A., 2009

Natural Care Series by Pat Coleby includes volumes for goats, horses, sheep, cattle, pets, and goat and alpaca, Acres U.S.A.

Natural Remedies for Animals Series by Mark Gilberd includes volumes for cats, dogs, goats, sheep, pigs, cows, horses, and poultry, CreateSpace Independent Publishing Platform

The Animal Desk Reference: Essential Oils for Animals, Melissa Shelton, CreateSpace Independent Publishing Platform, 2012

Grooming

How to trim cow hooves—www.youtube.com/watch?v=OkFOsz6P2Xw

How to trim goat and sheep hooves—www.youtube.com/watch?v=6ffU_cBjlsk

How to trim pig hooves—www.youtube.com/watch?v=03H23Zyitz4

How to trim chicken claws (nails)—www.backyardchickens.com/articles/trimming-your-chickens-nails-tutorial.64401

How to trim rabbit nails—www.thespruce.com/how-to-trim-rabbit-nails-1237208

How and When to Shear a Sheep—onpasture.com/2016/03/28/how-to-shear-a-sheep

Do-It-Yourself Fecal Parasite Counts

With a McMaster microscope slide—www2.luresext.edu/goats/library/fec.html

Using the modified McMaster fecal egg count—web.uri.edu/sheepngoat/files/McMaster-Test_Final3.pdf

With Epsom salts—www.goatbiology.com/fecalsolution.html

Kits and supplies:

    www.vetslides.com

    fecsource.com/shop

Kits and microscopes:

    www.farmsteadhealth.com/microscope.html

    eggzamin.com

Alternative Treatments

Treating Mastitis Without Antibiotics—eap.mcgill.ca/agrobio/ab370-11e.htm

Essential Oils as Dietary Supplements for Dairy Cattle—www.extension.umn.edu/agriculturedairy/feed-and-nutrition/essential-oils-as-dietary-supplements

Medicinal Herbs for Rabbits:

White Wing Rabbity, http://whitewingrabbitry.weebly.com/medicinal-herbs-for-rabbits.html

Rise and Shine Rabbitry, https://riseandshinerabbitry.com/2012/06/09/medicinal-herbs-for-rabbits

Integrated Parasite Management for Organic Dairy Cattle—www.nodpa.com/ParasiteManagement/Integrated_Parasite_Management_May_2005.pdf

Inclusion of Diatomaceous Earth in the Diet of Grazing Ruminants and Its Effect on Gastrointestinal Parasite Burdens—www.mtsylviadiatomite.com.au/sites/www.mtsylviadiatomite.com.au/files/Research/de_natural_dewormer_study_0.pdf

Effects of Regano (oregano essential oil) on Sheep and Goat Parasites—mofga.org/Publications/MaineOrganicFarmerGardener/Spring2010/Regano/tabid/1556/Default.aspx

Herbs as an Effective Tool in Coccidiosis Control—farmhealth.eu/news/herbs-as-an-effective-tool-in-coccidiosis-control

Herbal Parasite Management—landofhavilahfarm.com/loh/natural-raising/my-holistic-methods/herbal-parasite-management

Homemade Herbal Animal Dewormer and Tonic—libertyhomesteadfarm.com/herbal-remedies/homemade-herbal-animal-dewormer-tonic

Natural Goat Medicine—www.naturalark.com/natgoathealth.html

Chapter 9:
Keeping Them Safe

Peterson Field Guide to Animal Tracks, Olaus J. Murrie and Mark Elbrouch, Houghton Mifflin Co., 2005

Chapter 10:
Keeping Things Manageable

Keys to Successful Homesteading—http://northcountryfarmer.com/?page_id=1665

INDEX

PHOTO CREDITS

All photos from shutterstock.com except kinder goats on page 22 © Dan Tate.

Wood grain for chapter openers © marekeliasz

page 1: title wood grain © Madredus

page 12: farm with pond © Edward Fielding

page 16: Australorp chickens © Karin Jaehne

page 17: Hereford cow © visuall2

page 19: Holstein cow © VanderWolf Images

page 20: Boer goats © Muslianshah Masrie

page 23: East Friesian sheep © Bildagentur Zoonar GmbH

page 26: Tamworth pig and piglets © Mike Russell

page 28: New Zealand white rabbits © francesco de marco

page 32: Muscovy ducks © Perutskyi Petro

page 34: Narragansett turkey © Nancy Kennedy

page 36: Guinea fowl © Anna Ilieva-Alikaj

page 41: barn © photogal

page 41: coop © eurobanks

page 45: loafing shed © Sherry Saye

page 46: feeding pan and trough © Bearok

page 48: hay feeder © Sally Clarke

page 48: hay net © Undise

page 52: wood fencing © Mihail Pustovit

page 52: barbed wire © Frannyanne

page 53: chicken wire © makeitahabit

page 54: corral panels © vincent noel

page 61: Buffalo grass © kuruneko

page 68: shepherding © Linas T

page 72: raking hay © David Pereiras

page 93: rooster © tratong

page 113: bottle feeding © Craig Hanson

page 120: hen laying eggs © BePhumirat

page 122: pickled eggs © Bjoern Wylezich

page 130: hand milking © 7th Son Studio

page 154: root cellar © vagabond54

page 158: shearing sheep © Dalibor Sevaljevic

page 186: raccoons © Stephen B. Goodwin

page 188: llamas and goats © Jpecks19

ACKNOWLEDGMENTS

The book that you now hold in your hands wouldn't have been possible without the help of others, and I'm tremendously grateful for their encouragement and support.

To Dan, my husband and life partner, thank you for always being available to discuss ideas, read my day's work, offer suggestions, and give me a hug when I needed it.

To Shayna Keyles, Casie Vogel, and Molly Conway of Ulysses Press. Thank you for introducing me to the world of team publishing. Your availability and feedback have been invaluable.

And to my readers, whether of my blog or other books, a huge thank you. Your comments, enthusiasm, and encouragements are the reason I keep writing.

ABOUT THE AUTHOR

In 2009, Leigh and Dan Tate purchased on old farmhouse on 5 acres in the foothills of the Southern Appalachians. There they work toward simpler, sustainable, more self-reliant living through stewardship of the land and everything on it.

Leigh is the author of several books, including *5 Acres & A Dream The Book*, *Critter Tales*, *How to Bake Without Baking Powder*, and *The Little Series of Homestead How-Tos*.

She blogs at www.5acresandadream.com.